DATE DUE

JUL 6 '02			

A GUIDE TO
GAIA

A GUIDE TO GAIA

A Survey of the New Science of Our Living Earth

MICHAEL ALLABY

E. P. DUTTON
New York

First published in the United States in 1990 by E. P. Dutton,
a division of Penguin Books USA Inc.,
2 Park Avenue, New York, N.Y. 10016.

Published simultaneously in Canada by
Fitzhenry and Whiteside, Limited, Toronto.

Originally published in Great Britain under
the title *Guide to Gaia*.

Library of Congress Catalog Card Number: 89-85843

ISBN: 0-525-24822-6

1 3 5 7 9 10 8 6 4 2

First American Edition

CONTENTS

Preface   vii

1. The Earth Mother   1

2. Matters of life and death, and the
   two dog problem   14

3. Blue skies   28

4. Why the sea isn't boiling hot   44

5. Why can't you walk on water?   58

6. Derbyshire born   72

7. The sum of its parts   85

8. Red in tooth and claw?   98

9. The Earth is not a god   111

10. How planets die   126

11. A place for people   142

12. Physicians to a planet   157

Index   177

PREFACE

This book tells a story of adventure and discovery. Truly new ideas are rare, even in this modern age, and the idea I describe here is of a very special kind for it revolutionises the way we see and interpret the world in which we live. You might say it redefines the word 'Earth'.

It states that for most practical purposes our planet is a single living organism and its inhabitants, the countless species of plants and animals we see around us, may be likened to the organs of a body. The implications reach far and to many levels of understanding. They provide us with a means for assessing threats to the natural environment; but they do much more, for if living species may be described as 'organs', what kind of an organ are we? We have to review our own, human, place in the world, with all that means in philosophical and theological terms.

What is known as 'the Gaian hypothesis' began in the late 1960s when its principal author, James Lovelock, was working in the United States for one branch of the space programme. I first encountered it as a short article he wrote for *New Scientist* in the early 1970s. A few years later I met him while working on another book, quite unconnected with Gaia, but since then our collaboration, on two books and several magazine articles, has been entirely concerned with Gaian projects. Indeed, such is the attraction of the theme that I have found it refuses to be excluded from anything I write that is connected, even remotely, with environmental matters. It may not be identified by name but its influence is pervasive. It is that kind of an idea.

James Lovelock and his colleagues who have contributed to the central theme are eminent scientists. The theme is scientific and should be described and debated principally in scientific terms. But not everyone is familiar with the way scientists argue a case or with the technical terms they use, and so many people may be excluded from the discussion. This scientific idea is too important and much too interesting for it not to be available to everyone and I believe it can be described in plain, everyday English. That is what I have tried to do here. I assume you have no knowledge of science and where the technical terms are important I hope I have explained them fully.

I also have a second task. It is important to state, clearly and in non-technical language, what the Gaian hypothesis is, but it is no less important to state what it is not. A powerful idea of this kind may be misunderstood, and may have been misunderstood already by some people. In the chapters that follow I outline the science of Gaia and its implications, but I also discuss what I might call the symbolism of Gaia, of which there are two kinds. The first is legitimate, and arises from the name itself and its mythical associations. The name is used as a metaphor, a device to help us understand a scientific concept. Taken too literally, however, it can generate a second, illegitimate symbolism in which Gaia becomes an abstract, supernatural person, a god, and the object of 'worship' by modern pseudoreligious cults. Such deification is harmful, to the idea and to those who adhere to the cults, and I go to some lengths to warn against such wrong interpretations.

This denial of certain misinterpretations leaves a gap. Each of us carries around a mental picture of the world and of our place in it. If the picture is changed, and the Gaian idea may change it, we are bound to start searching for our place within the new picture. The need is psychological and quite real. I explore it in Chapter 11, and suggest, fairly lightheartedly, a part humans may be playing in the drama.

The final chapter, in practical terms perhaps the most important in the book, shows how the concept can be applied to environmental problems. The difficulty here consists mainly in classifying the issues that present themselves. How are we to distinguish the serious problems from the trivial? We need a method, if for no other reason than to help us in allocating limited resources, and a method must have a logical basis. The Gaian hypothesis supplies such a basis.

Many scientists have contributed to the Gaian hypothesis and many now support it, but its core has evolved over the years from the vision and detailed work of James Lovelock. In acknowledging the fact this book becomes a tribute to him, but its interpretation of Gaia is mine. He has read it in draft, chapter by chapter as it churned from the computer, to ensure that what I have written makes scientific sense and does not contradict his hypothesis, but he may not wish to associate himself with some of my more fanciful speculations. I absolve him from those and emphasise that any errors the book may contain are mine and not his.

1
THE EARTH
MOTHER

We are blessed, or cursed, with a capacity for
understanding many things. Because of this we are driven
to comprehend the world in which we find ourselves, to
make sense of what we see, of the network of relationships
that affect us. We make pictures, maps to guide us. And
we cannot tolerate riddles; we play games with them, but
always the only purpose of the games is to find solutions.
Questions cannot be left unanswered. We must worry
them, pick at them, turn them this way and that, until, at
last, all is made plain and we can rest from our labours.

Today we have a powerful technique for solving riddles.
We can examine our world in great detail, recording what
is and what happens, and storing the results of our
observations. Because technology has supplied tools that
can be used in this task we are able to explore the
intricacies of things far too small to be seen with the
unaided human eye, and we can even step outside our
world and view it from space. Then we can analyse our
observations to detect patterns in them, and advance
possible explanations for those patterns. The explanations
allow us to make predictions, and in most cases predictions
can be tested.

We might observe, for example, that salmon no longer
spawn in a river where once they were common. We might
find the salmon had also deserted certain other rivers, and
that would encourage us to examine the rivers to see
whether something had happened to change some aspect
of them and whether all of them had been changed in the
same way. This might lead to the further observation that
factories were pouring liquid wastes into all the affected

rivers, while other rivers, still favoured by salmon, had few or no factories along their banks. So we might predict that if the factories stopped discharging their wastes into the rivers, or removed certain harmful substances from the wastes before discharging them, then the salmon might return. The prediction would not be difficult to test.

THE PRACTICE OF SCIENCE

We call our riddle-solving technique 'science', and this is a book about science. More particularly, it is about a scientific idea, one attempt at an explanation.

'Science' can sound forbidding, and if you seek to practise it, to be a scientist, you will have to spend years mastering many difficult concepts and a daunting vocabulary. Measuring the flow of rivers, analysing the water they carry, and examining closely what goes on inside the body of salmon, all in very precise detail, are complicated, both to perform and to describe. This fact should not be allowed to exclude the non-scientist, however, for it is not difficult to describe and understand the chain of thought the scientist has followed without going into detail.

The word 'science' comes from the Latin *scientia* and it means 'knowledge'. That is all. Scientists work in a certain way to acquire knowledge, but it is the knowledge, the fruit of their work, that matters. We can understand that without becoming scientists, just as we can enjoy listening to music or watching movies without having to become musicians or moviemakers.

Science is meant to illuminate. There is nothing mysterious or threatening about it, and although 'science' and 'technology' are often confused it is worth remembering that they are quite separate and often quite unrelated. Indeed, many scientific advances have resulted from explanations of the principles underlying devices made years earlier by engineers — technologists — who knew only that they worked.

RIDDLES WITHIN RIDDLES

This, then, is a book about science, but it tells a story
rather than presenting a scientific text. It is also about
riddles and puzzles of the kind we cannot bear to ignore,
simply because they are puzzling. They are deep and
ancient puzzles and the attempted explanations I shall be
describing are by no means the first.

They are embedded, these riddles, like Chinese boxes,
one within another, so that each solution reveals a new
puzzle. How do living things reproduce? Answer that and
you will need to know why offspring resemble their parents
so closely. Answer that and you will have to discover the
precise means by which heritable traits are transferred
from each generation to the next. Answer that and you may
find yourself wondering how that means first appeared.

Our own origin and that of the world itself has always
been the biggest riddle of all. Solve that, and perhaps we
will understand all that flows from it. So, since long before
the dawn of history, people have sought explanations with
all the means at their disposal, and have presented their
explanations using the language and images available to
them.

Myths are not merely tales invented for the sake of the
telling, as entertainment for winter evenings. They tell of
familiar, homely beings and events, but at a deeper level
they describe what is dark and strange. Consider, for
example, this ancient account of our origins.

There was a vast, universal, unbroken darkness and in
the darkness there hovered Nyx, the great black-winged
bird, the only being existing but uncreated. Nyx laid an
egg. The egg hatched and from it sprang Eros, who flew
away on golden wings. The two halves of the eggshell
sprang apart. One became Uranus the sky. The other
became Gaia, the Earth.

Darkness, the Earth, the sky, a bird and its egg are
familiar enough to everyone, and the supernatural being
with golden wings suggests that something marvellous
happens. The myth is not literally true, in the way a

newspaper story is supposed to be true, but we must not discount it on that ground, for it is profoundly serious. Even today it survives to influence the way we think about the world. It is not 'true', but there is truth in it.

That search, for the origin of all things, forms part of the wider search for better maps, more accurate and more detailed pictures of the world to guide us safely through it. We need to know where we may go, what we may do, and those places and actions we must avoid. Again, for most of our history, the map has existed in the form of stories. Things, both animate and inanimate, were perceived as having a spiritual dimension. They were closely associated with beings on another plane of existence, so the stories concerned the relationships among those beings and between them and humans. In time, as the Gaia myth developed, the lesser beings became more prominent while Gaia and Uranus retreated into the background. There are far more stories of gods and goddesses, fairies, elves, trolls, gnomes, goblins, witches and sprites than there are of Gaia and Uranus, but the originals, the archetypes were still there. Many of the lesser beings are no more than Gaia's representatives, embodying one or other of her many aspects.

MOTHER EARTH

Her? Gaia has always been considered female. She is the Earth Mother. It is not too hard to see why. The Earth, the ground on which we stand, produces from itself plants, the food we eat. It supplies the stones, timber and clay with which we build our homes for shelter and safety. It supplies the ores from which we smelt metals to make our tools. It supplies almost everything we use. The idea is ancient, not only in the history of our culture but also psychologically. As babies, we perceive first of all our mothers. They supply everything, we are wholly dependent on them; they are, for that early time, our entire world. Fathers are also important, but it is only later that the developing child recognises their role.

The story in which Gaia and Uranus are formed from the shell of the egg produced by the bird Nyx comes to us from the Orphics, followers of the philosopher and priest Orpheus, who may or may not have existed as a real person. Orphism contains many elements derived from the beliefs of ancient Egypt, and the first Orphics, or perhaps Orpheus, probably encountered them in Crete from where they spread to Greece. In the Egyptian version it was a Nile goose that laid the cosmic egg.

There are other versions. Athenagoras, a Greek Christian who lived in the second century, probably in Alexandria, wrote of a snake that emerged from the water and that had three heads, one of a lion, one of a giant who may have been Herakles or Chronos, and one of a bull. The giant created an egg that split in two, one part forming the sky, the other the Earth.

Water often appears in such stories. The Egyptian bird was a water bird and the snake may represent a river, long and narrow, twisting and turning, and altogether snakelike. Water, after all, is hardly less important than dry land, and those who dwell in areas prone to drought cannot avoid being keenly aware of the fact.

The Gaia stories are essentially Indo-European and the earliest inhabitants of Europe emphasised water and air rather than the Earth. Their 'Mother' was a bird or a snake, either an inhabitant of the sky from where water comes, or the snake river, another source of life-giving water, and an obvious reminder of milk. The images also contain a strongly human element; the bird and the snake were partly human, and female, in form.

The stories were not confined to the Greeks and Egyptians. They also occur in the far north of Europe. Nor was it the Egyptians who invented them, for they are much older than that. Certainly they are older than the invention of agriculture, and images of the Earth Mother are older still. They have been associated with people who lived in Aurignacian and Magdalenian times, more than 30,000 years ago. It seems fairly safe to assume they are as old as humanity itself.

They are also universal. The Earth Mother, or Great Mother, features in the ancient beliefs of the Yoruba of west Africa, of the Melanesian peoples of the Pacific and, sometimes in a more sinister form, throughout the Americas.

IMAGES AND LIVING REMINDERS

The earliest representations of the Earth Mother that have survived are small figurines made from stone. Usually the breasts and belly are huge, the head eyeless and sometimes only suggested, and very often the buttocks are grotesquely large. The imagery may be partly sexual, but only partly. The Mother is often depicted seated, and early representations of Gaia herself, one of the versions of the Earth Mother, show her half-buried in the ground, her womb, below the surface, becoming the Earth itself.

Our language, the origin of the words we use and the ways we use them, reveals much about the history of our ideas. It is in our language that Gaia reveals her continuing presence most strongly, and the seated image is part of it. She sits on the ground and is therefore associated strongly with the Earth, but, more than that, by sitting she is declaring her ownership. In Britain, even today, a landed aristocrat will sound only slightly archaic if he refers to his large country mansion and the land he owns around it as his seat. A German aristocrat would use a very similar word, and talk of his *Wohnsitz*. In German the verb *sitzen* means to sit, but *besitzen* means to own, and in both English and German sitting suggests ownership, control and authority. Members of a company board or a committee have seats and their head sits in the chair. In German the word for chairman is *Vorsitzer*, the one who sits in front.

The imagery goes further. The Earth Mother sits, but she can also become a seat. She is associated with caves, reminiscent of her womb, but also and very powerfully with mountains. The mountain can become her seat, or throne, but while seated she may take others on to her lap. The child who sits on the Mother's lap has been accepted, is protected, is especially favoured above all the other children. So the man who sits on the sacred lap is similarly favoured above all others, becomes the son of the Earth Mother and the acknowledged ruler in the land. Kings ascend or mount the throne as though it were a mountain and as though the throne were sacred. By ascending the throne they take possession of the Earth. The name Isis, one of the Earth Mother's manifestations, means seat or throne and she bears its symbol on her head. In some cults the throne itself is worshipped. So, in Britain if not in more democratic America, there are aristocrats with seats and monarchs, not to mention senior bishops, who ascend and then sit on the throne.

There are others, beings more divine even than princes, who claim the right to sit on the lap of the Earth Mother. Such a divine being becomes a god, and is usually male. The male god, more familiar to us today than his mother, is a relatively recent representation of other qualities, and his ascendancy, in societies that are heavily dominated by males, has rather obscured his origins. Yet the mother figure survives, even in the modern world, and if the image of the divine virgin who gives birth to and then protects and nourishes a male divinity sounds familiar, this is not coincidence. There is much of Gaia in the Virgin Mary.

This is not the only way Gaia survives in our everyday speech, nor even the most obvious one. All of us use her name frequently, and especially if we are teachers or students in school. There is more than one version of the name itself. I call her Gaia, but the name can also be spelled Gaea, or simply Ge, which is also the Greek word for Earth, and a very common prefix to words that are connected with the Earth. Geometry is measurement, originally of the Earth; geology is the study of the rocks of the Earth; geophysics and geochemistry of the physics and chemistry of the Earth's interior; geomorphology of the surface features of the Earth and the way they form; geography of the Earth's surface; geochronology of the history of the Earth as determined by the dating of rocks; geomagnetism of the Earth's magnetic field; and there are many more, some of them grouped together in what are now known as the Earth sciences. When the growth of a plant is influenced by gravity, as when a stem grows upwards and a root downwards, it is called geotropism; the study of politics in relation to the geographical relationships of countries is geopolitics. The full list of ge-words is very long, and their connection with the Earth, with Gaia, means new words are needed to describe similar studies of other planets. The study of the 'geology' of Mars is called are-ology, for example, from Ares, the Greek god of war whom the Romans renamed Mars.

THE TERRIBLE MOTHER

I live in Cornwall, the long, narrow peninsula in the far southwest of Britain. It is a place of moors, deeply incised wooded valleys, farms, high sea cliffs, rocky coves and sandy beaches. It is also a place of mines and their spoil heaps, for minerals have been taken from here since Roman times. Cornish people know a lot about some aspects of geology, especially those from which you can earn a living.

As I walk in the countryside, surrounded by a vast wealth of wild flowers and insects, and sounds of birdsong, the wind and the sea, it is easy to become sentimental about Gaia, to imagine her as a benign Mother who cares deeply about all living beings, including me. But if I think that, I am profoundly mistaken. The wind on the clifftop can suddenly change direction and pluck people away, then drop them hundreds of feet on to the rocks below. The tranquil sea contains currents that carry swimmers far from shore, where they drown. Storms from the Atlantic can wreak havoc. The rescue services form an important and highly valued part of our community and every year wind and ocean claim human lives. Gaia has little concern for people. The Earth that is her womb is also a grave; the life-giving waters will all too readily swallow and digest us.

The old storytellers knew this well and had no illusions. The Earth Mother was also the Terrible Mother, pursuing, ensnaring and devouring her offspring aided by her lieutenants — hardship, hunger, disease and war. She is the flowers of the field, the birds of the air, but also the hungry Earth, the coffin, the vulture. She is Isis, Ishtar, Artemis and Sophia, and she is also Hekate, Kali and the Gorgon. In the story of Hansel and Gretel she is the witch whose house is made from chocolate and candy but who eats children.

Her most sinister manifestation occurred in the culture of the Aztecs. Theirs was a patriarchal society, apparently dominated by the male god of the Sun and dedicated to light, but there was also a figure called the Snake Woman and it was to her that human sacrifices were made. In Aztec Mexico, war against neighbouring peoples was ceaseless and essential to maintain a constant supply of prisoners to be fed to the Snake Woman. In Mexican art the Earth is not friendly. It devours everything.

The earlier beliefs, in which the Earth Mother was the dominant figure, gave way, but only partly, to a religion centred on a male god. Among many North American Indians, probably influenced by Aztec beliefs and customs, political power may have resided among the men and the principal gods may have been male, but internal affairs were often under the control of the old women. In earlier times the women, and the Earth Mother, had more formal power, but in some tribes a warrior could become a hero by fighting and overpowering the Terrible Mother. This transference occurs in many parts of the world, however, and is certainly not confined to America.

THE LIVING EARTH

Since long before humans began recording their stories in any formal way, the image on which all later beliefs were founded was that of the Earth as female, at once provider of all sustenance and destroyer, but above all alive. The world itself was living.

This is the central feature of the ancient idea that modern science has revived. The Earth, Gaia, is itself a living organism. Like the old Gaia, the living Earth is at once benign, in that you and I are part of it and sustained by it, and terrible, in that we are not essential to its well-being. Humans are dispensable and if we choose to destroy ourselves, or some catastrophe not of our making should overwhelm us, the new Gaia is no more likely than the old one to intercede and save us.

The vast bulk of the Earth is made from inanimate rock, a cosmic boulder, coated in places with a thin film of water. Life clings precariously to its outermost surface, like a blush of mould on the skin of a grapefruit. How can that boulder be alive, in any sense of the word?

We owe the revival of Gaia principally to one man, James Lovelock. He is central to my story and most of the ideas I describe originated with him, so I will have more to say about him and his ideas. He has faced this apparant paradox, of the living boulder, and answers it by comparing the world with a large, old tree, say a giant redwood. The tree is clearly alive. No one can doubt it. It has leaves (its needles), takes up water and nutrients, and one day it will die. You cannot die unless you have been alive. Yet if you examine the tree closely you will find that most of its bulk is accounted for by the main trunk and branches, and, apart from a very thin layer, they are nothing more than dead wood. The tree lives, but more than nine-tenths of it is made from non-living material. It is not so unreasonable, then, to describe the Earth as living, even though it is made mostly from non-living rock.

Lovelock is not the first scientist to think of the Earth as being alive, though he has taken the idea much further than any of his predecessors. James Hutton, the 18th-century Scottish geologist, often described as the father of geology, took a similar view. Hutton was trained as a physician and only later turned first to agricultural science and then to the study of the Earth itself. He once said, in 1785 in a lecture to the Royal Society of

Edinburgh, that the Earth should be regarded as a 'superorganism' and it should be studied by the science of physiology. His reasons have a distinctly modern ring, for he likened the movement of nutrients through the soil into plants and animals then back into the soil, and the movement of water from the oceans to the land and back to the oceans again, to the circulation of the blood.

There were others. Rather more than a century ago an independent, self-educated scientist from Kharkov, Yevgraf Maximovich Korolenko, also maintained that the Earth is a living organism, and he passed on this idea to his cousin, Vladimir Vernadsky, who later became an eminent Soviet scientist. The idea was heard, but ignored because it seemed romantic, improbable and vague, and it led nowhere. Even if the idea were true, of what use was it?

IS THE EARTH SICK?

In fact the idea may be a great deal of use. Hardly a day passes but we read in our newspapers or see on our TV screens reports of environmental problems. Poisonous industrial wastes kill fish and contaminate drinking water. The unwise use of pesticides kills plants and animals we would rather preserve. Manmade chemicals are damaging the ozone layer high above our heads. We are altering the world's climate by burning coal, wood and oil. Tropical forests are being cleared to supply us with timber and to produce beef, while the citizens of the formerly forested countries live in the direst poverty amid the ruins of what should have been untold natural wealth. The list is endless, and no sooner has one fear been aired than another appears. How are we to evaluate all these alarms? How can we know which are genuine, which imagined, which serious, which trivial? Yet we must know, must make decisions, for we are told that our very survival is at risk and we must take action.

A physician, facing a patient complaining of symptoms and expressing grave fears, will begin by making a thorough physical examination, but the examination is possible only because much is known about the construction and functioning of the human body. Knowing how it should work makes it possible to recognise malfunctions. That is the basis of diagnosis, and until a diagnosis has been made no treatment can be prescribed. What if we were to regard the world in the same way? What if we were to consider it as a whole, a distinct, discrete entity, and try to find out how the parts relate to one another, how the whole thing works? If we could do that, then the environmental alarms would seem like symptoms of an illness. We could examine them in the context of the whole organism, discover their underlying cause, evaluate their seriousness, and, in the end, prescribe remedies that are precise, appropriate, and involve the minimum of possibly harmful interference.

It is the approach Hutton recommended in the 18th century but until now it was not possible. Now, perhaps, it is. At least we can begin to consider it. That is what the new concept of Gaia attempts.

THE NEW GAIA

Clearly, the new Gaia differs from her old manifestation, subtly but profoundly. It may be that our ancestors believed literally that Gaia had an intelligence. The new Gaia does not, and perhaps it is better to explain it as a metaphor. Gaia is not an intelligence, not some kind of superhuman being. We cannot talk to her, reason with her, even pray to her, and expect to be heard, for there is nothing there to hear us.

Rather, the new idea is that if you take all the living things on the planet together it is possible to regard them as a coherent whole, like Hutton's 'superorganism'. This superorganism takes over the management of its inanimate environment, on a global scale obviously, and maintains it much as the human body manages and maintains its own internal environment. It does not plan this, and neither particular organisms nor the totality of the superorganism act in order to achieve a predicted outcome. It just happens, inexorably and inevitably. You can say Gaia, or the living Earth, exists; perhaps you can say something about the way it works; but that is all you can say. I repeat, because the point is important and I must emphasise it, there is no consciousness at work, no planning, and there are no goals to be attained.

In the course of the next few chapters I shall explore some of the ways in which living things regulate important and vast planetary processes and as I do so I shall produce entertaining and intriguing puzzles by questioning some very commonplace things, things we all take for granted. Why is the sky blue, for example? Why is the sea cold? How can anything live on dry land or, for that matter, in the oceans?

It is not with such puzzles, though, that my story begins, nor is it with such puzzles that the development of this new view of the Earth began. It began with a much more fundamental question, related to the most ancient of puzzles. What is the difference between something that lives and something that does not, and how can you tell one from the other? Suppose there are two planets, one supporting life and the other not. How can you tell which is which? This is where the search for Gaia began, and it is the proper place to begin my story.

2
MATTERS OF LIFE AND DEATH, AND THE TWO DOG PROBLEM

The best riddles are those with a sting in the tail, the ones that are not as simple as they look. Try this. There are two dogs, one alive and the other dead. How do you tell the difference between them? The answer is simple, of course. You say 'Walk!' in a clear voice and (assuming it understands English) one dog will become hysterical with excitement and impatience, while the other will remain still, its feet pointing resolutely at the ceiling. If you prefer to be a little more technical you might look for a heartbeat and breathing in each of the dogs. After all, the dog that looks dead might be only asleep and deaf.

At first sight this might seem a perfectly satisfactory solution. But is it? You have managed to distinguish one dog from the other, but you have said very little about the difference between the two. What difference is there? They are made in the same way, have similar skeletons, internal organs, body fluids, skin and fur. There are no parts missing. Analyse them chemically and you will find they are made from the same substances. So why is it that one of them falls over every time you try to set it on its feet?

WHAT IS LIFE?

The riddle, you see, is trickier than you may have thought. In fact it raises a very serious philosophical and scientific question. Since the only apparent difference between the two dogs is that one lives and the other does not, the difference turns on the presence or absence of life. What is life? It is not a substance. You cannot weigh or measure it. In everyday conversation we might talk about someone being 'full of life', as though that person had more 'life' than some other people, but this is a metaphor, a kind of verbal shorthand. Life is not a quantity. You cannot have more or less of it. If you have 'it' you are alive, without 'it' you are dead and, while you can be close to death as life ebbs away, you cannot really be half dead. Have you noticed that no one is ever described as being a quarter dead or two-thirds dead? You can halve life, but even metaphorically that is as far as you can go in dividing it.

It is not as though the question were unimportant or had no practical relevance. It matters to doctors, for example, who may need to know when they can remove organs for transplantation. It matters to people dealing with major accidents and other emergencies. It matters to the relatives of the gravely ill, and it matters most of all to the patients themselves.

It matters to us, too, but in a slightly different way. Gaia is very much associated with living things, and with life itself. As I will be using it, in its scientific sense, the name Gaia means 'living Earth' or, to be more precise, 'Earth considered as a single living organism'. Gaia is neater. Perhaps it helps us hide from the fact that it is not at all easy to say what life and living mean.

IF YOU'RE ALIVE, YOU DO THINGS

People have been trying to define life for a very long time. One of my jobs is to compile scientific dictionaries and I, too, faced the problem of definition when I was working on *The Oxford Dictionary of Natural History*. I fudged, like everyone else, and defined 'life' in terms of what living things do — eat, excrete, reproduce and so on. I am in good company. *The Shorter Oxford Dictionary* devotes half a page to the subject, but the best it can do, as a first definition, is to report, ineffect, that life is the quality of being alive. To ordinary people like us this difficulty in defining life is inconvenient, but to biologists, the life scientists whose business it is to study life, it is acutely embarrassing, though you will not find them admitting it. They never attempt a definition and never use the word if they can avoid it.

In the case of our two dogs, then, we can distinguish one from the other, so we can know which of them is alive and which dead, but we do it only by observation of their behaviour. Living things behave, they do things; dead things do nothing. As to the real difference between them, the presence or absence of something we call life, we can say nothing. In this deeper sense the apparently simple riddle has no answer.

It is all most unsatisfactory to those of us with tidy minds. We like riddles to have answers and stories to have endings. Happily, the Gaia concept can help. It does not lead directly all the way to a definition of life, but it does take us several steps further in that direction. Indeed, the search for life is where it all began.

STAR GAZING

On 4 October 1957, Soviet engineers and scientists launched the first manmade satellite, Sputnik 1. It circled the Earth, bleeping contentedly and to most of us unintelligibly. We all heard it on our radios, saw pictures of it, listened to experts discussing its significance, and we reacted emotionally. Some of us were excited, exhilarated at this first human step, albeit by proxy, to the very threshold of our own planet, to the boundary separating us from the rest of the universe. The door had been opened, as it were, and we could gaze through it. Others were frightened, in those otherwise dark Cold War days, at the awesome techological power Sputnik represented, and at its military implications. The two sets of emotions merged and the US space programme was born with two guiding motives: to explore, and to forestall the unequal militarisation of space.

The scientific study of space and of stars and other objects in space is the province of astronomers and cosmologists. There are many amateur astronomers who observe the night sky and whose observations make a valuable contribution to our knowledge of what is there, but interpreting those observations, which is what professional astronomers spend most of their time doing, rapidly becomes impenetrably mathematical. Cosmology, the study of the origins, structure and laws governing the universe, is even harder to grasp. You cannot even begin to understand cosmologists in any detail until you have mastered the theories of relativity and most of the concepts of modern physics, and the mathematics are truly formidable. Most of us depend for information on popular books and articles. These may be excellent, but they do not allow us to enter their mysteriously mathematical worlds directly, to explore for ourselves.

LITTLE GREEN MEN

We have augmented the science that is passed on to us with space fiction, and most writers of space fiction sprinkle the universe with planets and then populate planets with intelligent living beings. After all, fictional places are not very interesting unless fictional people visit them, and if the fictional places are away from Earth it is reasonable to suppose their inhabitants and way of life will be unfamiliar to us. So space fiction is full of alien civilisations and, hoping that life may imitate art, we would like there to be alien civilisations out there in the real universe. If we cannot find a civilisation, at least let us hope to find life.

The idea of other worlds, and life on them, is not new. Anaxagoras, a philosopher who lived in Athens probably around 428 BC, taught that the Moon had mountains and he also believed it had inhabitants. This was much too attractive an idea to be allowed to wither, and although it fell from favour during the centuries when people believed the Earth was the centre

of the universe, it was never quite lost. In our own century
books, short stories, films, radio and television have
allowed it to flourish.

In principle it may be true. There may well be life, even
intelligent life, elsewhere in the universe. We have sent
messages on our unmanned spaceships, designed to be
understood by the inhabitants of planets that orbit distant
stars, and SETI, the Search for Extraterrestrial
Intelligence, monitors the radio frequencies constantly in
search of signals that might contain messages from other
civilisations. Clearly the idea is taken seriously enough for
a little money to be invested in it.

SEARCHING FOR LIFE

This being so, it is hardly surprising that when excursions
were planned to the Moon and to the other planets in the
solar system the search for life was one of the objectives, if
a minor one. We knew, of course, that the Moon has no
atmosphere, no liquid water, that it is alternately
extremely hot and extremely cold and that while the Sun
shines directly on it the surface is bathed in intense
radiation at all wavelengths, including gamma and X-rays.
It is an unpromising environment and hardly one in which
to start the search. In any case the Moon is close enough to
Earth for it to have been examined very thoroughly, over
many years, with Earth-based telescopes, and no sign of
life has ever been observed. True, we see only one side of
the Moon because it spins on its axis more slowly than the
Earth does so it is always the same side that faces the
Earth, but there was never any reason to suppose the side
hidden from us is any different from the one we can see
(and we know now that it is not).

Mercury, the innermost planet, is very close to the Sun
and even less hospitable. Nothing can live there. Jupiter,
Saturn and the other outer planets were too far away to be
visited in the early days of the programme. Attention
centred, as it had centred in most of the fiction, on Mars
and Venus. Venus is almost the same size as Earth and its

surface is obscured at all times by what is usually called 'cloud'. Cloud seems to suggest water, and for a time Venus looked promising. Unhappily, closer examination of the 'cloud' revealed it as more like thin haze, but haze that rises to a great height above the surface, and it is made not from water but largely from sulphuric acid. There is no water to speak of in the atmosphere and none as a liquid at the surface. The atmospheric pressure at the surface is about 90 times what it is on Earth, and the surface temperature is high enough to melt lead. Venus is no place to live, and we now know that nothing lives there.

That left Mars, the red planet, the place where canals were once supposed to exist, the home of the pugnacious degenerates H.G. Wells had invade us in *The War of the Worlds.* The canals proved illusory, but the planet does have an atmosphere, what look like polar icecaps, and weather with seasons. There was hope.

In the spring of 1961, when space exploration was in its infancy and many wise people were saying it was a waste of time and money because most of its aims were impossible, James Lovelock was invited to work for NASA, at the Jet Propulsion Laboratory, in California, where they were preparing for the manned exploration of the Moon. His first job was to design instruments that would measure and analyse materials found on the surface, but before long he was set to work designing instruments that would analyse atmospheres and that could be sent to other planets.

It was not long before his thoughts began to turn to that ancient quest for alien life. The quest had become real enough. Venus, Mars and the whole of the rest of the solar system were either within reach or soon would be, and the first question to which the tax-paying public demanded an answer was the old, familiar one. 'What lives there?' That was when Jim hit the two dog problem.

WILL YOU KNOW IT WHEN YOU SEE IT?

According to most of the books and movies, when you come across aliens there will be no doubt about it. The problem of knowing what to look for hardly exists. If anything lives out there, quite probably it will attack you. Or it will run away. Or it will just lollop along taking no notice. Mostly it will make funny squeaking noises by way of communication, but when you finally get through to it the conversation will be in English (unless the Russians have been there first, presumably).

The trouble is that most writers are constrained by their experience, which covers a wide diversity of living things but all of them on the same planet. Anyone can tell the difference between a dog and a human, but the skeletons, internal organs, lungs, blood vessels and nervous systems of each work in exactly the same way. Humans and dogs are made of the same substances, more or less in the same proportions. The differences we see are quite overwhelmed by the strong similarities. If an intelligent alien met a dog and a human he could tell they were different but he would know in a few minutes that they came from the same planet. The lichens that coat rocks and trees, even the humble green algae that appear as slime on wet stones, use much of the same chemistry that we do.

When you visit a different planet why should you expect living things to resemble those on Earth? They may have developed entirely different solutions to their problems, may use entirely different chemistry, be made of different substances, and there is no reason at all to expect them to look even remotely like any living thing on Earth.

How would you cope, for example, with a world in which living things looked exactly like rocks, were made just like rocks, felt and tasted just like rocks, and never moved, at least while they were being watched? How would you know there was anything living at all and, if you came to suspect that some of the rocks were alive, how would you tell which they were? This is the two dog problem, and to solve it you have to think hard about what you mean by 'life'.

BY THEIR DEEDS YE SHALL KNOW THEM

Lovelock felt there had to be an easier, more certain way of searching and, in collaboration with others, he started not with any attempt to define 'life', but with a consideration of the things living beings do. If something lives it must be able to repair its own body and probably it grows for at least part of its life. For this repair and growth it needs materials and also the energy with which to process the materials, to convert them from the stuff of the planet it inhabits to the stuff of its own body. When it completes its processing of materials there will be a residue of waste of which it must rid itself. A living thing, then, processes materials. It takes them from one place, uses them, and disposes of wastes in another place. When it does this it modifies its surroundings. After a little while those surroundings are no longer in the condition they were in at the start.

This opens up a possibility. We may not know much about 'life', but we know quite a lot about the laws of chemistry and physics. If we can draw up a list of the chemical substances at or near the surface of a planet, and if we know the energy that is beaming down from the planet's star, it is possible to calculate all the chemical reactions that are likely to occur. This leads to a reliable prediction of the substances we should expect to find and the proportions of each. If the environment is not in its predicted chemical state, if it contains substances the laws of chemistry and physics suggest should not be there for example, then we must look for alternative explanations. One of those explanations may be that something on the surface is processing materials, and we have already agreed that processing materials is what living beings do.

LOOK AT THE SKY

Where should we start looking? Without being in the least specific about the kind of life that might exist, we can say that some places are more promising than others.

Chemical reactions occur most quickly and most prolifically in a fluid environment and especially in liquids. So look for a planet that has liquids on its surface.

True, there are some reactions that occur in solids. They take place in rocks as they cool after having moved close to the surface from much deeper levels where they are molten, but this is a special case. No one should expect to find living beings inside hot rocks because reactions there are relatively short-lived, lasting only until the rocks solidify completely. Even if something could start to live under such conditions, and some scientists believe life on Earth began with complex mineral crystals, a different and probably liquid environment would be needed to sustain the process later.

The temperature is also important. The complicated substances that living beings are likely to use break up into simpler substances at high temperatures. The addition of heat energy allows the groups of molecules from which they are made to break free. This is what happens when we cook food, and no one would expect a living thing to survive a thorough cooking. So the surface of the planet must not be too hot.

It must not be too cold either, because the reactions that lead to the production of those complicated substances proceed very slowly, or not at all, at very low temperatures. And, of course, the liquid containing them must not freeze. Life might appear on a very cold planet, but it would take a very long time indeed and time is not unlimited. Planets do not last for ever. All in all, life in a very cold climate is rather improbable.

We should look, then, for a planet that has liquids at or just below its surface. Such a planet will also have an atmosphere. It must have an atmosphere because the temperature at which liquids vaporise (i.e. their boiling point) depends on the pressure exerted on them. In Tibet the traditional drink is tea, drunk, they say, while it is still boiling. Tibetans who travel to lower altitudes from their high plateau have sometimes tried to make and drink their tea the way they like it, with painful consequences. The higher the altitude, and so the lower the air pressure, the lower the temperature at which liquids boil. Where there is no air at all, and therefore no air pressure, liquids cannot exist because they vaporise at once; under such conditions, the temperature at which a solid melts is the same as that at which its liquid form boils.

If substances are being taken from a liquid and then processed, at some point most of them are likely to exist as gases and to enter the atmosphere, so the atmosphere is the best place to look for these substances. So far as visitors are concerned this is very convenient, as the atmosphere is the outermost part of a planet and is the easiest part to examine. Provided you can get close enough to the planet to be able to see it through powerful telescopes, there is no difficulty in telling quickly whether or not it has an atmosphere, and some measurements and calculations will tell you the atmosphere's total volume and mass, and its chemical composition.

THE LIFE DETECTOR

There is no need to visit the planet. If you wait until, from where you are placed, the planet and the star around which it orbits are a good distance apart, you can measure the amount of energy from the star and pass its radiation through prisms to break it down into its spectrum, its constituent parts. Then you wait again until the star is behind the planet, aim your instruments at the planet and use the prisms again. As the light from the star passes through the planet's atmosphere some radiation will be absorbed, some will be reflected, some refracted (bent), and the spectrum will be different. Because different substances affect light in different ways, a comparison between the two spectra will tell you the composition of the atmosphere, both in substances and in the proportions of each substance. Working on this principle, modern instruments can analyse atmospheres very precisely and can register the presence of very small amounts of minor constituents. If the Lovelock line of reasoning is correct, and such an analysis can be used to detect the presence or absence of living things, we might as well call the instruments a 'life detector'.

Clearly there are living things on Earth, and it has been proved that nothing lives on Mars or Venus, so perhaps a little space fiction will help to elucidate things. Suppose a starship from some distant star system were to visit our solar system in search of alien civilisations. What might the scientific officer find?

As the ship moved into this region of the galaxy the Sun would appear to be just one of many rather ordinary stars. When the ship was closer, but still hundreds of millions of miles away, powerful telescopes would reveal the fact that the Sun has a system of nine planets, some of the planets with satellites (moons). The crew might decide it was worth a closer look. Closer still, they would dismiss Mercury, the innermost planet, because it has no atmosphere and surface conditions are too extreme for anything to survive. They would also dismiss the outer, giant planets, at least at first, as being too massive, too cold, or both. Their interest would centre on three planets that seemed more promising — counting outwards from the star, numbers two, three and four, the ones we humans call Venus, Earth and Mars. Beyond Mars lies the asteroid belt, a region of thinly dispersed lumps of rock of varying sizes, remnants of a very small planet that failed to form. The asteroid belt would be a convenient place to park, undetected because from a distance the ship would look like just another asteroid, but close enough to examine the three planets.

WHAT WOULD BE FOUND?

The crew would begin by measuring the volume and mass of each atmosphere. Knowing that all the planets formed at the same time, from the same collection of raw materials, they would also know that chemically they should all be rather similar, and a few analyses of nearby asteroids would tell them what those raw materials were. So, knowing the amount of energy each planet receives from the star, knowing the size of each atmosphere, and knowing the chemical substances from which the planets are made, our space scientists could start making calculations. These would tell them what the composition of each atmosphere should be, according to the laws of chemistry and physics. When they had completed their calculations they would begin analysing the atmospheres to see whether their measurements matched the predictions.

The calculations would show that chemically the atmospheres of all three planets should be almost identical. There should be at least 95 per cent carbon dioxide, between about 2 per cent and about 4 per cent nitrogen, very small traces of oxygen ranging from none on Earth to about one-tenth of 1 per cent on Mars, and traces of argon. The average temperature at the surface of each planet should be controlled by the distance between the planet and the star and the density of the atmosphere. On Mars, the outermost planet of the three and with the thinnest atmosphere, the surface temperature should be about −53 °C (−63 °F), on Earth about 300 °C (570 °F) and on Venus about 460 °C (860 °F).

Then they would start the analyses. Mars and Venus would be found to have atmospheres and surface temperatures very similar to those predicted for them. Since they can be explained wholly by chemistry and physics alone, nothing extraordinary is happening and it is very unlikely that anything lives on either planet.

EARTH IS VERY DIFFERENT

Earth, however, is nothing like the predictions. Its atmosphere is 79 per cent nitrogen, 21 per cent oxygen, a mere 0.03 per cent carbon dioxide, and it also contains a small amount of methane, which should not be there at all. The average surface temperature should be about 300 °C (570 °F), but in fact it is about 13 °C (55 °F). This is so extraordinary as to demand explanation.

The atmosphere is highly unstable chemically. Indeed, it is something of a chemical impossibility. Nitrogen should not be present as a gas, methane and oxygen cannot coexist because they react to form carbon dioxide and water, and where has all the carbon dioxide gone? The scientific officer would report to the captain that in all probability the third planet out from the star supported life abundantly. As I shall explain in the next chapter, he could go further and tell the captain a few things about the kind of life the planet might support. He might even deduce that it supports intelligent life.

THE REBIRTH OF GAIA

In the 1960s James Lovelock and his colleague, philosopher Dian Hitchcock, used this reasoning, and analyses that had already been made of the Martian atmosphere, to predict that Mars would be found to be lifeless. In 1975 the two Viking landers confirmed the prediction.

Such is science, however, that the answer to one question raised others. It was possible to distinguish planets that support life from those that do not, but what did the differences imply? Clearly, the wide disparity between the atmospheric composition and surface temperature predicted for Earth and those that actually exist result from the activities of living organisms, so this must be something else that living organisms do. They consume, excrete, reproduce, and as they do so they transform their local surroundings. Taken together, though, the entire mass of all the living organisms there are or that have ever been have transformed utterly the entire atmosphere of the planet. Other investigations suggest that they have also transformed the oceans. And we need only look from any window to see how they have transformed the land surface; from my window, where I should see bare rock, there are trees, herbs, grasses, a street, houses, cars, and birds flying overhead, some of them hunting for insects of which there are countless millions, some of them almost too small for me to see.

It is no exaggeration to say that on Earth the living beings have taken over the planet, not only in the sense of having colonised every part of it but in the much more important sense of having altered its chemistry beyond recognition. They are running the planet, in a coordinated way and on such a vast scale that we might just as well suppose the planet itself to be a single living organism. In the next few chapters I will try to explain how this management operates and what it all means.

Some years later, and back in England once more, James Lovelock found himself living in the same village as the novelist William Golding and the two became friends. As they walked together in the countryside, discussing an idea that by that time had been outlined in a few short articles published in scientific journals, it was Golding who suggested reviving the ancient name Gaia to describe Lovelock's vision of an Earth that does much more than sustain life. It is, literally, alive.

3
BLUE SKIES

When I was a boy I tried quite hard to find out why the sky is blue. Asking grown-ups was a waste of time. They stared at me as though I were crazy, or told me to find something useful to do, or simply pretended not to hear. It mattered, though. Where I lived it rained a lot of the time. A sunny day with a clear sky, when they let you go out to play without a stuffy, restricting raincoat, was something to be celebrated, when time itself might slow right down while you explored, or threw or kicked a ball around, or went swimming, or rode your bike, or just lay on your back in the grass. There were meadows then, full of wild flowers. You had to keep looking at the sky, just in case it might change its mind and decide to rain after all, so I could hardly avoid noticing its colour. These days it is usually paler. The really deep blue is even more of a rarity than it was all those years ago. This is not my fancy; it really is so. It is a matter we will need to think about later.

So why is the sky blue? A long time later I discovered two answers, or, more accurately, one answer but two ways of expressing it. I found the complicated version first, and I have to confess I did not think much of it. It told me that molecules of air that are small in relation to the wavelength of light scatter the incoming sunlight in such a way that more blue than red light gets through to the surface. I liked the second, simpler answer much better. It said the air contains a lot of oxygen, and oxygen is blue. It is very pale blue, so if you had a jar of it you would see no colour, but if you look through a lot of it, as you do when you stand on the ground and stare up into the sky, the blue shows.

I was satisfied with that until I learned that so far as anyone can tell Earth is the only planet where the sky is blue. The first photographs from the surface of Mars showed a beautifully pale blue sky, but then they corrected the colour to what it should be, a no less beautiful, but strange, pale pink. If anyone were foolish enough to visit Venus, in the few seconds remaining to them while they cooked they would see a pale yellowish-brown kind of sky. It is the oxygen that makes our sky unique, at least in the solar system.

We take the air for granted but, as I suggested in the last chapter, this is a mistake. It is very odd and it was not always the mixture of gases it is today. I was right to get excited about the blue sky. It is odd because the whole of the solar system formed together at the same time and from the same raw materials, so the three inner planets, Venus, Earth and Mars, which are close together and must have shared whatever was around at the time, ought to be pretty much the same. To understand what the raw materials were, where they came from, and how it is that Earth has grown so different, it is best to summarise the story from the beginning.

THE BIRTH OF A STAR

It all began with a cloud and a star, a star much bigger than our Sun. The cloud was cold and diffuse, and it was drifting peacefully around the galaxy doing nothing in particular. Most probably it consisted mainly of hydrogen and helium, with small amounts of other light elements, such as lithium, because those are the most common elements in the universe as a whole, formed very soon after the 'big bang' that started it all. The star, on the other hand, was busy.

Stars form from clouds of gas whose particles are drawn together by their own gravity. As they fall toward the centre they form a mass of matter denser than the surrounding matter and as this core grows larger so its gravitational attraction increases because the force of gravity is proportional to the mass of the body exerting it. Near the centre of the core the mass of all the matter pushing inward produces huge, and constantly increasing, pressure. As the pressure increases, so does the temperature. When the pressure and temperature are high enough (the temperature must be about 100 million degrees Celsius) hydrogen atoms are squeezed together so hard they fuse.

The nucleus of any atom consists of protons, particles with a positive electrical charge, and neutrons, which are electrically neutral. The only exception is the hydrogen nucleus. It consists of just one proton, with no neutrons. Neutrons and protons can change one into the other with the release of a much smaller, electrically charged particle. Inside the nucleus, particles are held together by the strong force, which overcomes the electromagnetic force that makes bodies with a similar electrical charge mutually repellant. There are only four forces that govern the universe. The other two are the weak force and the gravitational force.

The strong force operates only over the very small distances inside an atomic nucleus. Outside the nucleus the electromagnetic force dominates, so nuclei, which are always electrically positive because of their protons, repel one another and it requires very large amounts of energy to bring them close together. Nevertheless, inside a star that is what happens because of the extreme pressures exerted by the gravitational force.

Each time two nuclei are crushed together, protons, neutrons or both are brought close enough such that the strong force binds them together, thus making a new atomic nucleus with more particles than either of those from which it was made. Having more particles makes it heavier. Altering the number of protons in an atomic nucleus changes its chemical characteristics and so converts it from one element into another. In this way a series of new elements forms, each heavier than the last.

Four hydrogen atoms (protons) fuse in a series of reactions to make one helium atom (two protons and two neutrons), but the mass of the helium atom is slightly less than four times that of a hydrogen atom. The lost matter is converted to energy according to Einstein's famous equation $E = mc^2$ in which the energy is equal to the lost mass multiplied by the square of the speed of light. The centre of the star heats up, heat is carried outwards by convection, and the star begins to shine.

The heat generates an outward pressure, as the centre of the star tries to expand. For a time — the 'main sequence' of the star (and the state our Sun is in at present) — the two pressures, gravity pushing inward and expansion pushing outward, are balanced. When most of the hydrogen in the core has been consumed, the temperature falls a little, the outward pressure is reduced, more matter falls inwards, the pressure increases again, and helium atoms are squeezed together to form carbon. In a star the size of the Sun that is as far as it goes, and smaller stars may get no further than 'burning' their hydrogen.

THE DEATH OF A STAR

If the star is bigger, however, the temperature goes on rising and the process continues. When the temperature reaches about 800 million degrees Celsius carbon atoms fuse to form neon. Still hotter and neon atoms fuse to form oxygen, oxygen atoms to form silicon, and silicon atoms to form iron (26 protons and 30 neutrons), each time releasing more energy. Other elements are also produced, all of them lighter than iron, but they do not take part in these fusion reactions. The particles that compose iron nuclei are very strongly bound together and forcing iron atoms to fuse calls for much more energy than is available at the heart of a star, so there the process ends. The star has used up all its fuel, contracts, and becomes a white dwarf, a burned-out star.

In the centre of a very massive star, however, one that is at least eight times the size of the Sun, by this stage there is a core of iron surrounded by a shell of silicon. The silicon is being converted to iron, so the core is growing constantly and, at this stage, very rapidly. The pressure inside the core goes on increasing until a limit is reached. The atomic nuclei cannot be compressed further, shock waves travel outwards, and in a chain of very complex reactions the star explodes, with energies high enough to produce all the elements heavier than iron. That is a supernova explosion. It lasts a fraction of a second and casts off the outer shell of the star, complete with its heavier elements. The cast-off shell travels outwards at a speed of around 10,000 kilometres a second, cooling rapidly.

THE FORMATION OF THE SOLAR SYSTEM

Let us now return to the cloud I described earlier. When the matter from the supernova explosion encountered the cold, diffuse cloud, the collision caused turbulence. Particles began to aggregate and so began the collapse that led, about 4.6 billion years ago, to the formation of the solar system.

The supernova remnants provided the solar system with its stock of heavy elements; there is no other way it could have acquired them. If our stellar ancestor had been a cloud of matter left over from the big bang, the solar system would contain little but hydrogen and helium. If it had been a star the size of our Sun it would contain no element heavier than carbon. The fact that we have iron, and lots of it, means we are descended from a star much bigger than the Sun, and the fact that we have still heavier elements, such as uranium and thorium, means the birth of our own star was preceded by the most spectacular kind of thermonuclear explosion the universe can produce.

The mixed cloud now consisted of gases along with particles ranging in size from fine dust to large boulders. As it collapsed in on itself, and began to rotate about its own centre, matter started to accumulate at certain locations. Almost all of the mass concentrated to form the Sun, with the planets as relatively tiny objects outside it. The inner planets formed as particles collided and were held together by their mutual gravitational attraction. The forming planets sorted out their ingredients, the heavier tending to congregate near the centre so the inner core of the Earth is made mainly from iron and nickel. Repeated collisions caused some heating and the decay of radioactive elements produced in the supernova explosion, mainly uranium and thorium, caused further heating, so the planets grew hotter, except at the surface where heat was radiated away into space and rocks remained solid.

The gases in the cloud formed an atmosphere around those planets whose gravity was strong enough to hold them. Then the Sun reached the stage in its development at which its hydrogen atoms began to fuse. Its furnace lit, the star began to radiate, and the early atmospheres, made from light gases, were heated, became less dense, and were swept away into space as though by a great hot wind. But already other gases were replacing them.

On the planets, material heated by the natural nuclear reactors deep below the ground erupted to the surface as volcanoes, ejecting the gases that accumulated to form a new atmosphere. On Earth, that atmosphere is believed to have consisted mainly of carbon dioxide, with a little hydrogen but no oxygen, and it would also have contained water vapour.

The water that forms the oceans may also have been erupted from volcanoes, although there is doubt about this. Some scientists believe it arrived, late in the formation of the planet, when the Earth was bombarded by huge boulders of ice. Comets are made mainly from ice, so this theory is plausible, if controversial.

WHY DOES OUR AIR HAVE SO MUCH NITROGEN?

Today the atmosphere is four-fifths nitrogen. Nitrogen gas is composed of molecules each of which is made from two nitrogen atoms bonded together very firmly. The strength of the bond between them means that unless something happens to supply enough energy to break it, nitrogen will not react with other substances.

The energy to break that bond comes mainly from lightning. Thunderstorms may be fairly uncommon in any particular place, but over the world as a whole they are very common indeed. Each stroke of lightning, which is really a huge electrical spark, makes some nitrogen (chemical symbol N) react with water (H_2O) to form nitric acid (HNO_3) and a little ammonia (NH_3). Both these are very soluble in water, so they are removed from the air in the rain that accompanies the thunderstorm. Once on the ground they react with substances in rocks and eventually form nitrates (NO_3), all of which are very soluble in water, so once dissolved the nitrogen is trapped. Since all water flows from the land into the oceans, the oceans should contain all the world's nitrogen. If nitrogen compounds are erupted from volcanoes, or manage to enter the atmosphere in any other way, they should be removed. So there might be a little nitrogen in the air, but Earth has far more than we would expect. The scientific officer on that starship parked out in the asteroid belt would find this very interesting.

In fact we know how our atmosphere comes to have so much nitrogen. It is the work of bacteria. To be more precise, it is the work of a group of what are called denitrifying bacteria, although nowadays the burning of coal, and ammonia given off by animal urine, also contribute to it. The denitrifying bacteria live in water, mud, and in soils, especially waterlogged soils, and they are everywhere. They live even in the crusts of algae that grow on the surface of clay soils in some deserts. Nitrate (NO_3) passes inside the bacteria, which derive their energy from a series of reactions in which the nitrate is reduced (oxygen is lost from it) to nitrite (NO_2) and then to nitrogen gas (N_2) or sometimes nitrous oxide (N_2O), also a gas.

The bacteria themselves cannot tolerate free, gaseous oxygen. Today other groups of nitrifying bacteria make gaseous nitrogen combine with oxygen, but to do that they need a plentiful supply of oxygen and in the early history of the Earth the oxygen was all firmly combined with other elements. There was a long period, therefore, during which denitrifying bacteria were able to prosper, deriving energy from reducing nitrate, but the nitrifying species had not appeared. Nitrogen was therefore released into the atmosphere faster than lightning could remove it, and so it accumulated.

As he sat puzzling over his measurements, the starship scientific officer would soon figure out that water vapour and lightning should remove all but a small amount of nitrogen from the air and that very special conditions were needed for the reactions by which nitrate could be broken down to release its nitrogen. He would suspect living organisms of being involved and would add this to the evidence he was accumulating to show that life on Earth was probable.

WHY SO MUCH OXYGEN?

Then he might turn his attention to all that oxygen, amounting to about one-fifth of the atmosphere and colouring it blue. The most likely source of the oxygen, he might reason, is the carbon dioxide (CO_2) he had found in the atmospheres of Mars and Venus and that he would expect to find on Earth. The trouble is, splitting carbon dioxide into its carbon and its oxygen molecules is difficult, and requires not only energy but also some very special chemistry, involving a catalyst. (A catalyst is a substance that makes a chemical reaction take place but is itself unchanged at the end of the reaction.)

The catalyst in this case is one of the complicated compounds called chlorophylls. Chlorophyll a, the more common of the two chlorophylls found in green leaves, has the chemical formula $C_{55}H_{72}MgN_4O_5$ (Mg is magnesium). The chlorophyll traps the energy of sunlight and then starts a series of reactions in which carbon dioxide and water are broken down, a simple carbohydrate (CH_2O) and more water are produced, and surplus oxygen is released as a byproduct. Carbohydrate molecules are then combined to make sugars, which supply the fuel to produce other chemical ingredients of living organisms. Photosynthesis, the word we use to describe the initial process, if far from simple and involves other complex substances such as ATP (adenosine triphosphate) and NADP (nicotinamide adenine dinucleotide phosphate). All these are made in special chemical factories inside cells, where the ingredients can be selected and brought together and the products concentrated and protected against random reactions with other substances that would destroy them.

That, then, is the source of the oxygen in our air. The chlorophyll is contained in special parts of plant cells called chloroplasts, and there is good reason to suppose that at one time chloroplasts lived independently of the plant cells in which they are found today.

The oxygen was not released by any of the big plants we see around us now. Such plants came much later. The oxygen-producers were microscopically small, single-celled organisms containing chloroplasts, or possibly the free-living chloroplasts themselves. Nor did the oxygen accumulate in quite the way nitrogen did. Unlike nitrogen, oxygen reacts readily with many elements, forming oxides. For a long time free oxygen oxidised other substances, and was consumed as fast as it was produced, accumulating as a gas only when there was nothing left at the surface with which it could combine.

The oxygen in the air is further strong evidence of living organisms.

METHANE, THE FINAL PROOF

The presence of so much nitrogen and oxygen is, therefore, strong evidence of the presence of life, and the scientific officer might well decide Earth was worth a closer examination. That examination would settle the matter beyond any reasonable doubt because the instruments would reveal small amounts, rather less than 2 per cent of the total, of methane.

Methane (CH_4) is a simple enough compound. The trouble is that it cannot survive in the presence of oxygen. We know methane principally as the main ingredient of natural gas. We burn it in our stoves and heating systems. When we do that the methane is oxidised in a series of steps leading to carbon dioxide and water as end products, with a release of energy, almost all as heat. But to get the reaction started we have to ignite the gas. We need at least a spark to raise the temperature of a few molecules, just to get things going, and, of course, we need a plentiful supply of the gas in a concentrated form. It is far from being concentrated in the atmosphere, and it will not ignite even with the spark of lightning flashes, but it oxidises all the same. The reaction is slower, that is all.

Once he has calculated the total amount of methane in the air, and the total amount of oxygen, the scientific officer can calculate how long it will take for the two gases to consume one another, leaving the oxygen somewhat depleted but removing the methane entirely. Only the methane is not disappearing. Indeed, at present the amount of it is increasing.

There is no way the oxidation of methane can be prevented, so something must be releasing methane into the air at least as fast as it is being consumed. On the face of it that presents no great difficulty. The raw materials are there. Carbon (C) can be taken from carbon dioxide, and hydrogen (H) from water. Unfortunately, it is much more difficult than it looks. If ordinary sunlight could supply enough energy to split carbon dioxide and water into their constituent atoms it would have done so billions of years ago, and neither carbon dioxide nor water could have survived on Earth or on either of its sister planets. Some extra chemistry is needed. In fact the same chemistry that is used to release oxygen in the first place, photosynthesis, involves splitting both compounds. Joining them together again to make methane is no easier, however. It is a reaction that proceeds in stages and at each stage the intermediate product is so unstable it would fall apart if it were exposed to the air and the reaction would get no further.

By this point in the story it will come as no surprise to learn that the methane is being manufactured and released by bacteria — very small, single-celled beings that live in places where gaseous oxygen is unknown. The methane is a byproduct of their own digestive systems. The chloroplasts break down carbon dioxide and water, and from these they make carbohydrates. When the photosynthesisers die they provide food for others and eventually some of it reaches the methane bacteria, living in dense, airless, sticky mud in such places as sewage plants, river estuaries and rice paddies, and in the stomachs and guts of most large animals. These bacteria are the last to feed on the remains of the photosynthesisers and in the course of obtaining the energy they need they join carbon to hydrogen and so manufacture methane.

The scientific officer will now be convinced that, taken together, the nitrogen, oxygen and methane in the atmosphere very strongly suggest the presence of living organisms. The chemistry of the planet is being manipulated on a vast scale and, having been perturbed, it is being prevented from stabilising itself.

It seems only fair to allow that his instruments are at least as good as those available to our own scientists, so we may as well see what else he can discover. Persuaded that the planet is inhabited, the next obvious question is: inhabited by what?

IS THERE INTELLIGENT LIFE?

Among the substances present in the air in extremely small amounts he might notice methyl chloride (CH_3Cl), produced by certain small plants and wood-rotting fungi, and the main source of the chlorine (Cl) in the upper atmosphere. He might also detect some other contributors to that upper atmosphere chlorine, strange substances that can be made only under conditions of temperature and pressure much higher than those he can measure. His instruments might well reveal the presence of chlorofluorocarbons (CFCs), made from carbon, fluorine (F) and chlorine, some of them with hydrogen as well. They are difficult to produce and it is almost impossible to make them react chemically with anything at all, so it is difficult to see what purpose they serve.

He would be forced to conclude they were made industrially, and industry implies intelligent beings. So his analysis of our atmosphere would have told him that, almost certainly, Earth is inhabited, and among its inhabitants there are some intelligent enough to have industries. Most people might think pumping CFCs into the air is not a particularly intelligent thing to do, but it all depends what you mean by intelligent and the scientific officer has to take a broad view.

THE DANGERS OF OXYGEN

At this stage I like to think of him sitting down (if they do that where he comes from) and trying to figure out how it all works. What effect on each other do the constituents of the atmosphere have?

I think he would start with the oxygen, because oxygen is so reactive and that makes it potentially dangerous. Substances containing carbon oxidise rapidly in the presence of oxygen, and rapid oxidation is a roundabout way of saying burning. That ought to worry the inhabitants of Earth, because according to his calculations they are all made mainly from carbon.

How readily things burn depends on how much oxygen is available and whether they can be ignited. Ignition is no problem on Earth. There is plenty of lightning and, quite apart from that, volcanoes erupt frequently, bringing very hot lava to the surface.

Fires must be commonplace on Earth, but they are tolerable because not everything is consumed. The atmosphere is about 21 per cent oxygen and that is not quite enough to start all the carbon burning spontaneously, but it is close. Were the concentration to increase to about 25 per cent, the carbon would all be turned into carbon dioxide rapidly, in one vast, worldwide conflagration. At 30 per cent all the carbon would burn even if it were soaking wet.

Could the concentration of oxygen increase? Well, under certain circumstances it might. The accumulation of oxygen originally occurred as a result of the huge proliferation of photosynthesising cells and it was some time before organisms evolved to tolerate gaseous oxygen, indeed to require it as a condition of their existence, to need it for respiration. When that happened the amount of oxygen in the air stabilised, as the newly invented process of oxygen-based respiration derived energy from the oxidation of carbon, thus consuming oxygen and releasing carbon dioxide. Green plants release oxygen, but when they die they decompose and decomposition involves oxidising the carbon in their tissues back into carbon dioxide. The combination of photosynthesis and respiration ensures that the amount of oxygen released is balanced by the amount recombined with carbon.

If there were a sudden huge increase in the overall amount of photosynthesis, however, there could be a surge in the concentration of oxygen in the air. It is not very likely, but it might happen if, for example, vast new land areas appeared, as they might if a new ice age locked up large amounts of water in the polar ice caps and the sea level fell dramatically, or if other climatic changes accompanied by an increase in the amount of carbon dioxide in the air stimulated plant growth on a global scale.

Happily, there are checks. Methane and oxygen destroy one another, so as long as the air contains methane, oxygen is being removed all the time. Fires themselves also contribute, in two ways. The first is obvious. When something burns, its carbon is oxidised to carbon dioxide, and this consumes oxygen, so reducing the amount in the atmosphere. The second is more subtle. When living or formerly living matter burns, the ash contains phosphorus. Phosphorus is an essential nutrient element and I shall say more about these later. The phosphorus in the ash washes eventually to the sea and in the sea it is a shortage of phosphorus that increases the rate at which carbon is buried on the sea bed (another matter I shall explain in the next chapter). The effect of transporting large amounts of phosphorus to the seas may be to reduce the rate at which carbon is buried, leaving still more carbon available to be oxidised. So if an increase in the amount of oxygen is large enough to trigger widespread fires, the fires themselves may help remove surplus oxygen.

The methane bacteria and the land-dwelling plants, then, are indirectly engaged in this aspect of management.

USES FOR OXYGEN

What if the air contained less oxygen than it does? It would not take much insight for a chemist to decide that living organisms use oxygen to oxidise carbon, a reaction that liberates energy. With so much oxygen there should be organisms capable of some very energetic activities. The scientific officer would advise the captain that, should he send a party of explorers to the surface, they might expect to find organisms that could move rapidly. There might even be some that could fly. If there were less oxygen in the air, say around 15 per cent instead of 21 per cent, organisms would move sluggishly and there could be no flyers.

Oxygen serves another useful purpose. It keeps the air reasonably clean. We think of atmospheric pollutants as substances humans release. We do release large amounts, of course, but still larger amounts are released naturally. Winds blowing across deserts collect dust, living organisms emit a range of gaseous compounds, and volcanoes release vast quantities of both dust and gases.

In our atmosphere, however, anything that can be oxidised will be. Once the reaction has taken place the resulting molecule is likely to be less reactive than it was, and the less reactive a substance the less likely it is to be poisonous. At the same time the addition of oxygen increases the size of a molecule, so there is a greater chance that it will fall or be washed from the air by the rain. Pollutants can accumulate to harmful levels locally, but the air itself makes it most unlikely that those of natural origin could do so on any large scale. Oxygen and methane are very useful to the living organisms that put them there and that now maintain them in constant proportions.

WHAT USE IS NITROGEN?

That leaves the nitrogen. It is so reluctant to enter into chemical reactions that despite its unkind German name of *Stickstoff*, 'stuff that suffocates', it is perfectly harmless.

It does no harm, but is it useful? It may be. In the first place it dilutes the oxygen. What makes oxygen a fire hazard is not so much the total amount as the proportion there is of it. When the air pressure is very low, as it is at high altitudes for example, people may die from lack of oxygen. They can avoid this by increasing the supply of oxygen available to them, either by breathing pure oxygen through a mask or by sealing themselves in an airtight cabin and using ordinary air to keep the air pressure at a tolerable level. Military aircrews use the first method, airline passengers the second, and both methods are safe. Combining them, on the other hand, so that air pressure in a sealed cabin is increased by pumping in pure oxygen and thus increasing substantially the proportion of oxygen in the air, is very dangerous indeed. The smallest spark could ignite the nearest carbon and then the people themselves would burn fiercely. 'Padding' the atmosphere with nitrogen removes the risk.

The large amount of nitrogen also increases the air pressure. I mentioned earlier that the temperature at which liquids boil decreases as the pressure under which they are constrained decreases. With our atmospheric pressure, water at sea level boils at 100 degrees Celsius (212 °F), but in high places like Tibet it boils at a much lower temperature because the air pressure is lower. If the nitrogen in the atmosphere were reduced beyond a certain level the air pressure would also be reduced and water would boil at ordinary sea-level surface temperatures, which would be inconvenient, to put it mildly. It might not mean we would lose our oceans, because the large amount of water vapour entering the atmosphere would increase the air pressure again, but substituting water vapour for nitrogen to maintain pressure would certainly mean much less liquid water at the surface.

The main consequence of reducing substantially the volume of the oceans would be to alter the world climate. Water heats up and cools down more slowly than dry land. During the summer the oceans absorb heat gradually and remain cooler than the large continental land masses. Air passing from the continents over the oceans is cooled, and helps to cool the next land mass it encounters. In winter the reverse happens and the oceans warm cold air from the continents. Reduce the amount of water in the oceans and temperatures over the continents would become much more extreme.

A LIVING PLANET

The scientific officer would not find any of this surprising. He would know the ways living things organise themselves and their planets. Once his observations, measurements and calculations had convinced him the planet was inhabited he would expect things to be much as they are.

The original atmosphere has been replaced entirely by one supplied by the living organisms themselves and, having produced it, they maintain it so its composition and total volume remain constant.

The atmosphere they have produced is the one that suits them best. It provides them with the conditions and gases they need. This is no accident. It is not that the atmosphere came first and the organisms adapted to it. The very first organisms must have adapted to the conditions they found, but that phase did not last long. They altered what they found to such an extent that only its position in the solar system would make it possible to recognise that Earth is still the same planet as the one that existed before it came to life.

There is one more puzzle I have not mentioned, and in some ways it is the most important, and most curious of all. If the original atmosphere consisted mostly of carbon dioxide — carbon combined with oxygen — and the oxygen is now free, what happened to all the carbon?

4
WHY THE SEA ISN'T BOILING HOT

Sea water is cold. At least, it is where I live. They say that in some parts of the world the water is pleasantly warm but around here, along the northeast shores of the Atlantic, hypothermia sets in quickly. People bathe in it in summer, but sessions are short, and in winter the fanatic year-round surfers wear wetsuits.

Taken together, the seas are also very large. They cover a little less than 71 per cent of the Earth's surface to an average depth of about 12,000 feet. The total volume of that immense basin, and therefore the volume of the oceans, is about 330 million cubic miles, an almost unimaginably vast amount of water.

It sounds so obvious to say the sea is cold and big. Everyone knows that much. No one can remember a time when it was any different. It has always been cold and big and we take those facts for granted. They are curious facts all the same. Strictly speaking, the sea should be much hotter and somewhat smaller than it is. Its large size and low temperature are the result of events that took place long ago, early in the history of the planet, and they have much to do with a very modern environmental concern — the greenhouse effect.

WHY THE SEA DID NOT FREEZE

When the Earth first formed, some 4.6 billion years ago, the Sun burned less fiercely than it does today. We do not know that from direct observation, of course, but from studies of other stars that are very like the Sun. Such stars begin to burn when their internal pressures exceed a certain value, and then they grow hotter at a fairly constant rate as they age. By measuring the present output of heat from the Sun it is possible to use this rate of change to calculate back through 4.6 billion years, to a time when the heat reaching Earth from the Sun was 25 to 30 per cent less than it is today. Because in those days the Earth received less warmth from the Sun you might expect that the climate was rather colder than it is now. Indeed, the calculations suggest that all water on the Earth should have been frozen and that it should not have started to melt until about 2 billion years ago.

No one knows what the climate of the early Earth was like, but one thing is certain. The water was liquid, not ice. This means the temperature at the surface cannot have been lower than 0 °C (32 °F) or higher than an improbable 374 °C (705 °F), which is the highest temperature at which water can remain liquid even if it is held at much higher pressure than exists today.

The reason scientists are so certain that water has remained liquid throughout the history of the Earth is that they have found and dated sedimentary rocks. As the name suggests, sedimentary rocks occur when solid particles settle out from water to form a layer of sand or mud on the sea bed and are converted to solid rock by being subjected to high pressures and temperatures. The processes by which the rocks form are not relevant to the present argument. What matters is that those processes begin with the erosion of earlier rocks, mainly by wind and water, into small particles, which then settle out from the water. It is quite impossible for sedimentary rocks to occur unless abundant water is available, and there are sedimentary rocks on Earth that are about 3.8 billion years old. Still older rocks may exist, but they have not yet been discovered. Meanwhile, 3.8 billion years is old enough to be convincing.

HOW OLD IS A ROCK?

How can anyone know the age of a rock? Dating is a scientific discipline in its own right, called geochronology, and it has developed rapidly in recent years as the techniques available to its practitioners have increased. Most of these now rely on radiometric dating, that is to say on calculations based on the rate of decay of radioactive substances.

The cloud of matter from which the solar system formed contained many atoms whose nuclei are unstable. They decay by losing nuclear particles, sometimes emitting gamma radiation as they do so. The decay involves only the nucleus of the atom and it is unaffected by pressure, temperature, or any chemical reactions that may be occurring in its immediate surroundings, and for any particular kind of atom it occurs at a constant rate.

While it is impossible to predict just when any individual atom will undergo a decay, if you take a large number of atoms it is possible to predict very precisely how long it will take for half of those atoms to decay. This is called the half-life of an element. If the decay involves the atomic nucleus losing neutrons the chemical behaviour of the atom will be unchanged, because neutrons are electrically neutral so the relationship between the atom, its (negative) electrons and neighbouring atoms remains unaltered. However, the mass of the nucleus will change and this can be measured. If the decay involves the loss of protons, which carry a positive charge, the chemical behaviour of the atom will change and one element will be transformed into another. The scientist wishing to date a rock sample analyses the rock and compares the amounts of different elements and the atoms of the same element but with different masses (different isotopes). Calculating the age of the rock is then a matter of mathematics.

Several elements can be looked at. Uranium, for example, decays through several isotopes, eventually transforming into lead. Thorium also decays to lead. Lead itself is stable but still decays through several isotopes, rubidium decays to strontium, and a method that has come into use in recent years measures the decay of samarium to neodymium.

The techniques are now very reliable and the dating of rocks is precise. There is no doubt, therefore, that those ancient rocks really are 3.8 billion years old, any more than there is doubt that they are sedimentary rocks. Their existence proves conclusively that nearly 4 billion years ago there was liquid water on the surface of Earth.

THE GREENHOUSE EFFECT

The Earth was more highly radioactive in those early days than it is now. This is obvious, because radioactive elements decay eventually to stable elements that undergo no further decay, so the longer the process continues the more the stock of radioactive elements is depleted. The decay process is what is called exponential, which means it works like compound interest, in this case running backwards. If you give a value of, say, 1,000 (units do not matter) to the total amount of radioactivity, then after one half-life it will be 500, after a second half-life 250, after a third 125, and so on. The decay proceeds at a steady rate, but the amount remaining declines rapidly at first and then more slowly.

Being more radioactive, the interior of the Earth was hotter. This would not have warmed the surface rocks very much but it does mean there would have been far more volcanic eruptions than there are now. Volcanoes eject many substances, among them carbon dioxide and water vapour. Estimates of the amount of volcanic activity and the amounts of carbon dioxide ejected from volcanoes lead to the conclusion that originally the atmosphere contained a great deal more carbon dioxide than it does today and that the carbon dioxide, along with certain other gases, produced a strong greenhouse effect. Far from freezing, the average temperature at the Earth's surface about 4 billion years ago was comfortably warm. Some calculations suggest it may have been around 23 °C (73 °F), others that there may have been 1,000 times more carbon dioxide in the atmosphere than there is now and that the sea surface temperature may have been close to 100 °C (212 °F). It cooled, though, and for most of the Earth's history the average surface temperature has remained close to 13 °C (55 °F), which is its value today.

I shall have more to say later about the greenhouse effect, because it is a modern environmental problem, and a very serious one, that has many Gaian implications. Since those implications extend back to the very infancy of the planet, and thus concern this part of our story, I had better explain briefly what the effect is and how it acquired its name.

The concept is not new. In 1863 the British natural philosopher John Tyndall (1820–1893) suggested that the temperature at the surface of the Earth is related directly to the amount of carbon dioxide in the atmosphere, and in 1896 the eminent Swedish chemist and Nobel laureate Svante August Arrhenius (1859–1927) calculated that tripling the amount of atmospheric carbon dioxide would cause the surface temperature to rise by 9 °C (16.2 °F).

The Sun emits radiation at all wavelengths, but most intensely in the short waveband which we recognise as visible light. The gases that make up the air are completely transparent to such short-wave radiation, as is the glass of a greenhouse (so long as it is clean). Light and warmth from the Sun heat the land and sea surface and when they become warm those surfaces also radiate heat. Provided the amount of energy radiated from the Earth into space is the same as that received from the Sun a balance is maintained and the Earth will become neither cooler nor warmer.

The radiation emitted from the surface is at much longer, infrared, wavelengths, however, and gases whose molecules consist of more than two atoms absorb infrared radiation, different gases absorbing at particular wavelengths. The radiation they absorb warms them and they start to reradiate it, in all directions. Some of this radiation escapes into space, some is absorbed by other gas molecules and warms them, and some is directed downward, back towards the surface. The gases therefore act like a blanket, allowing energy to pass inwards but trapping outgoing radiation. Glass is also opaque to long-wave radiation. This is part of the reason why the air inside a greenhouse is usually warmer than the air outside and it is why the atmospheric phenomenon is called the greenhouse effect.

Quite a number of past or present atmospheric gases exert a greenhouse effect. We think mainly of carbon dioxide (CO_2) because that is the most abundant one and its effects have been studied longest, but others include water vapour itself (H_2O), ammonia (NH_3) and methane (CH_4). If the Sun has been growing steadily hotter, but the temperature at the surface of the Earth has remained constant, while at the same time the amount of carbon dioxide in the atmosphere has declined, it is difficult not to conclude that it was the disappearance of the carbon dioxide that regulated the temperature.

EVIDENCE FROM ANTARCTICA

We need not jump to hasty conclusions, however. There is some hard evidence to consider. At the Soviet Vostok station in Antarctica scientists drilled more than 2,000 metres below the ice surface to extract cores of ice for analysis, and in 1987 they published the results. These trace the changes in air temperature over the last 160,000 years, as ice ages have come and gone, and also the amount of carbon dioxide in the air.

When you make ice in a freezer you start with liquid water and freeze it rapidly to make blocks of ice. This is not the way ice sheets form. They begin as snow, small ice crystals, sometimes joined together to make snowflakes. They settle loosely, with tiny air spaces between them. As more and more snow falls its weight crushes the underlying snow until it is packed together and turns into ice, but ice that contains innumerable tiny bubbles of air. Once buried, that air is sealed from contamination by later air.

Year after year more snow arrives, more ice forms, and the ice sheet grows thicker. By drilling below the surface, therefore, scientists can recover ice and its entrained air from previous years, and the annual falls of snow can be counted, much like annual growth rings in trees, so the ice can be dated. That is how past air can be sampled.

The ice contains a record of the temperature at the time it formed. There are two important isotopes of oxygen, oxygen-16 and oxygen-18, and two of hydrogen, hydrogen-1 and hydrogen-2, or deuterium. The proportions of all these are constant in the atmosphere, but not in water, where they vary according to the temperature. The colder it is the more oxygen-18 and deuterium the water contains. By measuring the relative amounts of these isotopes in the ice cores it is possible to trace changes in climate.

When the air bubbles were analysed for their carbon dioxide content this was found to be linked very closely with climate changes — so closely in fact that it reflected relatively minor periods of warming and cooling during the last ice age. The investigators concluded that variations in the amount of atmospheric carbon dioxide played an important part in causing the warming that heralded the end of ice ages and also played a role in the cooling that preceded ice ages, although other factors also contributed to the cooling.

At one time it was thought that ice ages were a fairly recent phenomenon and that for most of its history the Earth had been free of ice. This is now known to be untrue. Indications of at least 15 groups of past ice ages have been found dating far back into the Earth's history. Large rocks found in places to which they can have been transported only by glaciers provide evidence of ice ages even in the Jurassic and Cretaceous periods, from about 195 to 65 million years ago, long believed to have been times of warm climates and ice-free conditions. Scientists now believe that ice ages are the rule and that ice-free periods are uncommon.

WHERE DID ALL THAT CARBON GO?

It seems, then, that the atmosphere once contained much more carbon dioxide than it does now, and the removal of that carbon dioxide led first to a cooling of a rather warm Earth and then held climates fairly constant while the Sun grew hotter. Despite ice ages, it has never been cold enough for the oceans themselves to freeze, except locally in high latitudes and then only at the surface, nor hot enough to make life impossible. What happened to all that carbon dioxide? The short answer is that it was buried, largely as a result of the activities of living organisms.

Carbon dioxide is slightly soluble and a little of it dissolves from the air into rain water, turning the water into weak carbonic acid (H_2CO_3). The rain falls on rocks and moves across them and among the tiny spaces within and between them, and as it does so the carbonic acid reacts with compounds of calcium, silicon and oxygen in the rocks. Calcium and bicarbonate (HCO_3) are released and carried, dissolved in the water, eventually to the sea.

Once in the sea living organisms convert the calcium and bicarbonate into insoluble calcium carbonate ($CaCO_3$) from which they make their shells. When we think of shellfish the big ones come to mind, those we can see and handle and eat, but the great majority are minute, and always have been. Nor are they all what we usually think of as 'animals'. The oceans teem with coccolithophorids, minute plants that have shells made from calcium carbonate.

When these plants and animals die their bodies disappear but the insoluble shells sink to the sea bed where they form sediments. As the plates of the Earth's crust move in relation to one another, carrying the continents with them, eventually the sediments are transported to regions where one plate is moving beneath the edge of another. Much of the sediment is taken down below the crust, but some, compressed into solid rock, is pushed upwards to form mountains.

The process still continues. Many deep-sea oozes consist

mainly of the remains of coccolithophorids. In others, covering nearly half of the floor area of all oceans, about one-third consists of the remains of tiny shelled animals called foraminifera, mainly of the genus *Globigerina*, after which that type of ooze is named.

You need not study the sea bed, though, for the evidence is all around us. Find chalk or limestone rocks — and they are very common indeed — look at them carefully, and you are almost bound to find fossils, although later changes, such as those that transform limestone into marble, destroy the fossils. (Some fossil-bearing rocks are called 'marble' but they are not true marble.) These rocks are made from the shells of plants and animals that once lived in the sea. If you doubt that these rocks represent a vast store of carbon dioxide, sprinkle a few drops of dilute hydrochloric acid on them and watch them fizz as the reaction between the acid and the calcium carbonate releases a little carbon dioxide.

There is another mechanism at work removing carbon dioxide from the air. Green plants use carbon dioxide in photosynthesis. The carbon is incorporated into their tissues and subsequently into the tissues of organisms that eat plants. When the organism dies its tissues ordinarily decompose and the carbon is oxidised back into carbon dioxide, but there are situations in which decomposition is arrested. This usually happens in waters so rich in organic remains that the decomposers cannot keep up with the rate at which dead material is presented to them. Remains settle on the bottom and are buried and compacted by fresh remains in an only partly decomposed form. This is how coal and oil are formed, but organic remains also become incorporated in sediments that turn eventually into slates, mudstones and shales, sometimes in such large amounts that the rocks, called oil shales, can be exploited for fuel. As with the sea shells, some of these sediments are carried below the Earth's crust (the technical term is subducted) and others are crumpled upward to form new mountains.

Subduction is not quite the end of the story. Below the

rocks of the Earth's crust lies the mantle, a region where temperatures and pressures are so high that the rocks are very plastic and behave as liquids. In the mantle the subducted calcium carbonate reacts with silica (the oxide of silicon you can find on the surface as quartz) to form fresh calcium-silicate minerals with a release of carbon dioxide. The gas is held securely below the crust but when a volcano erupts, throwing out material from the mantle, some carbon dioxide escapes with it.

This completes the cycle. Carbon is erupted from volcanoes, passed back and forth between the air, green plants and water, some is buried and some of the buried carbon is erupted again to rejoin the process. Over long periods, the limestones, mudrocks, slates and shales are worn away by wind and rain and by reacting with acids that occur naturally, and their carbon, too, is returned to the cycle. The leaks from the carbon stores are quite minor, however, and according to some estimates about half of all the carbon ever released from volcanoes has been returned to the interior of the Earth.

The cycle is not wholly in balance, then, and in the remote past it was even less balanced than it is now. The original atmosphere was rich in carbon dioxide erupted from volcanoes. This means that in the early history of the Earth there were far more volcanoes than there are today, and eruptions were much more frequent. Carbon dioxide was being pumped into the air very rapidly at first, but the rate soon decreased and no sooner had the Earth formed than it began cooling.

There was a time when the Earth was lifeless. That, coincidentally, was when the volcanoes were most active. When life appeared the carbon began to be used to make living tissues. Organisms reproduced, evolved, spread all over the planet, and their total mass increased. No matter that their death and decay returned carbon dioxide to the air; their expansion used up far more carbon than that, and once they had colonised every last corner where some cell or other could make some kind of living, their total mass remained fairly constant. A vast amount of carbon was needed to make all that living matter, and every last molecule of it was taken from the air much faster than it could be replenished by the volcanoes.

WHEN DID IT BEGIN?

Despite the fact that today most of the land surface of the Earth is covered with grasslands, forests, and plants and animals of every kind, the biological part of the carbon cycle has always taken place mainly in the sea. The plants and animals whose shells formed so many of our rocks removed large amounts of carbon that was buried, but in the very early days, before such complicated organisms appeared, the expansion of photosynthesising cells was the principal mechanism for carbon removal.

Those cells are still there, and they are no less abundant today than they ever were. They are what sometimes make the sea look green. The smallest of them are called prochlorophytes and in 1988 a team of biologists from the Massachusetts Institute of Technology, the Woods Hole Oceanographic Institution and Harvard University reported their discovery of a new group. Each of these prochlorophytes is about 0.7 micrometres across (lie about 36,000 of them side by side and they would make a line 1 inch long) and the scientists found them at densities of more than 100,000 in every millilitre of sea water (nearly 60 million in a pint). Yet they are but one group among many living in the surface waters of the world's oceans.

Photosynthesis is almost as old as the planet itself. Fossils have been found in sedimentary rocks that are around 3,500 million years old, but there is other evidence as well. The carbon in carbon dioxide exists in two stable forms (isotopes), carbon-12 and carbon-13, differing in the number of neutrons in their atomic nuclei, and one unstable radioactive form, carbon-14. When carbon dioxide is involved in simple chemical reactions, as when it dissolves to form carbonic acid that reacts with substances in rocks, the relative proportions of the various forms of carbon are unchanged. In photosynthesis, however, the proportions do change because one of the first steps in the process uses carbon-12 in preference to carbon-13, so living tissues are enriched in carbon-12.

In May 1988 Manfred Schidlowski, of the Max Planck Institute for Chemistry in Mainz, described in an article in the British scientific journal *Nature* how he had analysed sedimentary rocks from Isua in western Greenland that were 3,500 to 3,800 million years old. He found them enriched in carbon-12, showing that photosynthesis was widespread at the time the sediments accumulated, and suggested that nearly 4 billion years ago some areas may have been saturated with single-celled photosynthesising organisms.

If photosynthesis was widespread nearly 4 billion years ago we cannot avoid the fascinating if slightly eerie implication that still earlier forms of life, of which we have no direct evidence, must have existed even longer ago, and that life appeared on Earth almost as soon as the Earth was completed and available for occupation.

Clearly, the large-scale removal of carbon dioxide from the air began almost at once because the climate became somewhat cooler. Around 2,300 million years ago it fell a little too far and there was an ice age. After that it recovered and from then on the temperature remained more or less constant as the Sun grew hotter. The living organisms, the great majority of them microscopically small and dwelling in the oceans, brought the climate under control and have been regulating it ever since.

An ice age is a dramatic event, or seems so to us because we live between ice ages, at a time when only a small part of the Earth's surface is covered by ice. In climatic terms, however, an ice age is quite minor. A change of just a very few degrees in the average temperature is enough to start or end one. It sounds paradoxical to talk of the climate being constant and at the same time to admit that ice ages occur from time to time, but the temperature change involved is so small that really there is no paradox.

WHY THE OCEANS ARE SO BIG

The appearance of life so long ago also explains why the oceans today are as big as they are. The word volcano suggests a mountain on dry land, like Mount Fuji or Mount St Helens, that explodes from time to time hurling great clouds of smoke, steam and ash into the air and, in some cases, rivers of molten rock cascading downhill. The picture is not wrong, but that kind of volcano is not typical. Most volcanoes are on the sea bed, not dry land, and they erupt into the water, not into the air. About ten times more carbon dioxide is erupted by submarine volcanoes than by dry-land volcanoes.

The rock erupted by submarine volcanoes is mostly basalt, which contains iron. The temperature at which it is erupted is high enough for the iron to react with the water (H_2O), forming an iron oxide and liberating hydrogen as a gas. Unless some other chemical reaction occurs to trap it, the hydrogen will bubble to the surface and into the air. There, being lighter than any other gas, it will rise to the very top of the atmosphere and vanish into space. The Earth's gravity is just not sufficient to retain hydrogen gas. Before life appeared that is what must have happened.

This process removes water and so we must assume that the oceans were once larger than they are now. Had the process continued, more and more water would have been 'destroyed' and its hydrogen lost so it could never form again. The oceans would have bubbled away into the cosmos. After more than 4 billion years they might well have disappeared altogether, and at the very least they would by now be small and shallow, pathetic puddles compared to their former selves.

When life appeared, however, a check was imposed. The production of hydrogen went on, and still goes on, but there are many living cells that can make good use of hydrogen and they trap much of it before it reaches the air. At the same time the photosynthesisers release oxygen. They release it below the surface of the sea as well as directly into the air, so the upper layers of water contain ample supplies of the dissolved oxygen that allows animals such as fish to breathe. Hydrogen that bubbles through sea water without being trapped by cells must encounter oxygen sooner or later, and if it meets no oxygen in the water it will certainly meet it when it enters the atmosphere. Mix hydrogen and oxygen together and they combine to form water. Water cannot escape from the Earth, partly because its molecules are heavy enough to be retained and partly because almost all the water vapour condenses or freezes, and falls back to the surface, before it can rise high enough to escape.

The sea is thus colder and bigger than it would be if the Earth were lifeless, our climates are closely regulated to keep them within tolerable limits, and the regulators are living organisms. Most consist of a single cell far too small to be visible except with the help of a powerful microscope, and most live in the upper layers of the sea. If Gaia exists, and you can liken the planet to a single living organism, then these tiny single cells are the equivalent of the mechanisms in the human body that maintain its constant temperature.

5
WHY CAN'T YOU WALK ON WATER?

You ought to be able to walk on water. This talent should not be restricted to very rare, very special individuals. All of us should be able to do it. Perhaps actually walking on water is asking a bit too much, but at the very least we should be able to sit on the surface without sinking. When you walk the whole of your weight presses down through the sole first of one foot and then the other, and it is quite a concentration of pressure. When you sit your weight is distributed over a much larger area (some of us being more amply supplied in this department than others), so the pressure on each square inch of the surface supporting you is much less. Water should be able to bear that much.

The water has to be sea water, naturally. There is no way you and I could walk on the surface of a river or freshwater lake, but sea water is different. It is denser because of the salt it contains, and there is one sea, the Dead Sea, where you can almost sit on the water. You must have seen photographs of rather overweight gentlemen floating comfortably on their backs, fat cigars at jaunty angles in their mouths, reading newspapers. I expect they are really actors, hired by the local tourist board to drum up business, because it has to be more comfortable to read the newspaper sitting in a chair than lying flat on your back. All the same, actors or not, there they are. They are people, big, heavy people, and they float.

The Dead Sea is unique in its ability to float the corpulent. If any old sea could do it there would be no point in hiring actors to publicise the fact.

The Sea has several names, but 'Dead' is the one most widely used. As it suggests, floating newspaper readers apart, nothing lives there. At any rate, there are no fish or visible plants, although there are single-celled organisms adapted to survive in one of the harshest environments on Earth. The reason, of course, is that the Sea is exceedingly salty. Among its alternative names are the Salt Sea and the Sea of Lot, referring to the Old Testament story of Lot and his unfortunate wife, in which salt figures large.

HOW DO THEY MEASURE SALTINESS?

How salty is very salty? For that matter, what is salt? The dictionary definition states that a salt is the compound formed when an acid reacts with a base. The acid contains hydrogen, whose atom carries a positive electrical charge, and in the reaction the hydrogen is replaced by another positively charged atom, usually a metal. Common salt is sodium chloride, a compound of the metal sodium and chlorine, and sea water contains large amounts of common salt. It also contains many other salts, but in smaller amounts, including compounds of iodine and bromine as well as of chlorine.

If you fill a shallow pan with sea water, filtered to remove grains of sand and other solid particles, then heat it over a fire, the water will evaporate, leaving behind a whitish, crystalline deposit of salt. It is a tedious way to obtain a commodity you can buy in any supermarket, but it is salt. Indeed, it is sea salt, containing the full complement of salts rather than being pure sodium chloride. Some people believe it is better for you than supermarket salt.

When common salt dissolves in water its sodium and chlorine separate, so it is a little misleading to think of salt water as consisting of water with molecules of sodium chloride distributed evenly throughout it. It is really water in which charged atoms (ions) of sodium (positive ions) and chlorine (negative ions) move about independently of one another, freely and randomly.

Salinity is defined as the amount of common salt in one kilogram of water when all the organic matter in the water and all the carbonates have been converted to oxides and all the bromides and iodides (compounds of bromine and iodine) have been converted to chlorides (compounds of chlorine). They are not really converted, of course. This is simply an assumption that makes the calculation easier. The concentration of salt in water is rather difficult to measure directly so it is usually measured as the concentration of chlorine, called the chlorinity, which can be determined by a routine laboratory process. The resulting value can then be converted quite simply into the salinity. For historical reasons the final value is expressed not as a percentage (parts per 100) but as per mille (parts per 1,000), with a symbol like a percentage sign but with an additional zero in the denominator (‰).

Measured in this way, the salinity of the oceans ranges from 32 to 36 per mille, with an average of about 35 per mille. The Dead Sea is more than five times saltier than the oceans. At the surface its salinity is 195.4 per mille and at a depth of 250 feet, where denser, saltier water lies beneath the less dense surface water, it is 266.6 per mille. The only large expanse of water that is even saltier than the Dead Sea is the Great Salt Lake in Utah, whose salinity is around 270 per mille. A few organisms manage to survive even there, including some algae (single-celled plants) and other microscopic organisms, but also a species of shrimp and two species of flies whose larvae are aquatic. There are other relatively salty seas, but none to compare with these two; the salinity of the Persian Gulf and Red Sea sometimes exceeds 40 per mille, for example. Other seas are much less salty; at times the salinity of the Baltic falls to 1 per mille, so it is almost fresh water.

WHY YOU CAN'T DRINK SEA WATER

If it were a bit cleaner you could drink the waters of the Baltic without coming to much harm, but everyone knows you cannot drink ocean water. Indeed, many people have died from thirst while surrounded by water, with no land in sight, a suffering described most graphically by Samuel Taylor Coleridge in 'The Rime of the Ancient Mariner':

> Water, water every where,
> And all the boards did shrink;
> Water, water every where
> Nor any drop to drink.

Clearly, humans cannot drink salt water, not even water with as little as 35 per mille of salt, which is not very much when you think about it. If you drink such water the most likely consequence is that it will make you vomit. If you persist, and do not vomit, you will begin to dehydrate. Your body will start to lose the water it has.

This fate is not confined to humans. Although some can tolerate more salt than others, all living cells have a range of salinities within which they can survive. If they are exposed to much higher or much lower concentrations they will die. Too much salt dehydrates them, too little salt and they fill with water until they burst. Dissolved sugars, and indeed solutions of any kind, have the same effect, but salt solutions are by far the most common.

The reason for this susceptibility to very strong and very weak solutions lies in the construction of the containing membranes of a cell. A cell is completely enclosed, but it cannot be totally sealed. It is a tiny chemical factory where substances enter from outside to be used either as raw materials to supply energy or in the manufacture of the substances from which the cell itself is made, so it can repair or reproduce itself. Inevitably, this chemical processing generates wastes and these must be removed from the cell.

The membrane enclosing the cell must therefore allow certain substances to enter and other substances to leave. Substances can enter in various ways. Solids or liquids may be engulfed by the cell wrapping itself around them. The enclosing cell membrane bulges inward, like a pocket, until its outer edges meet and join to reform a continuous coating, turning the pocket into a completely contained 'purse' whose membrane is then removed. Other substances enter because they bear an electrical charge opposite to that inside the cell and are attracted and allowed to pass through the membrane. Entry ceases when the charge inside the cell is equal to that outside. Wastes are expelled through the membrane, often as crystals.

The membrane also has extremely small pores. If you add a quantity of salt water to a quantity of pure water, after a time the two waters will mix so thoroughly that the resulting salinity is somewhere between that of the salt water and the zero of the pure water, and the salinity will be the same throughout the liquid. The sodium and chloride ions, moving freely and at random, will have distributed themselves evenly. However if you separate the salt and pure waters by a membrane with pores so small that they will allow water to pass, but not sodium or chloride, water will pass through the membrane, but in one direction only, from the pure water to the salt water, diluting the salt water. It will go on doing this until all the pure water has disappeared or until the membrane bursts. If the two liquids are both salt solutions, but of different concentrations, the process will continue until the concentrations on either side of the membrane are equal. A membrane of this kind is called semipermeable and the process is called osmosis, from the Greek *osmos*, meaning 'push'.

Osmosis exerts a strong pressure. The movement of water will cease only when the pressure in the dilute solution, on the side of the semipermeable membrane out of which the water is moving, equals the osmotic pressure in the concentrated solution on the other side of the membrane. However, cell membranes are fragile, and cells will burst, due to extra water being forced in by the osmotic pressure, or collapse, due to water leaving the cell, long before that point is reached.

The simplest way for a cell to remain whole and functional while bathed in a fluid is for the solution inside the membrane to be at the same strength as that outside so no water passes in either direction. Many cells manage this, but there are alternatives. Cells that live in fresh water usually contain solutions stronger than the water surrounding them, so they take in water until, in the case of most plants, their own walls become sufficiently rigid to prevent further intake or, in the case of animal cells, they start actively to pump water out.

The cells in our own bodies, and in those of all animals, are separated from the environment outside the body but are bathed in body fluids, and in most cases the solutions inside the cells are of the same strength as the body fluids that surround them. The exceptions, the cells whose internal solutions are markedly different from those outside, are able to pump substances in and out as required, but only within limits. Exceed those limits and even these hard-working cells must perish.

This is why you need mineral salts in your diet, and also why an excess of them is harmful. Your body needs them because they are raw materials for the construction of more complex substances. Cells that are exposed to an outside environment they cannot regulate also need them to maintain their own integrity, to prevent death by osmosis.

But if you drink sea water your body fluids will come to contain excessive amounts of salts. This will cause water to drain by osmosis from cells bathed in those fluids, i.e. the water passes across the semipermeable membranes from the relatively dilute cell contents to the relatively concentrated body fluids. The cells will be damaged, eventually they will die, and you will suffer dehydration, the loss of fluid. I am much too sensible ever to have tried it, but legend holds that as you drink more and more sea water your thirst will increase instead of being assuaged. Meanwhile, the disruption of your normal body chemistry will affect your brain cells and you will go mad. Soon after that you will die. It sounds a dismal way to go.

LIVING WITH DANGER

The Gaian point is that all living things have to live with
this hazard. If the fluid they inhabit becomes too salty or
insufficiently salty they are doomed. A very few organisms
manage to tolerate extremely salty conditions, many can
tolerate fresh water, but very few of them can tolerate
wildly fluctuating salinities. Estuaries, for example, where
fresh water and salt water meet, are tough places to live.
Some fish, such as salmon and common eels, are able to
move between fresh water and salt water, but most
organisms stay in one environment or the other. Salt and
fresh water do not mix very readily, so it is possible for
some sea fish to move up-river with the tide by staying in
the stream of salt water, passing river fish that keep
themselves to the fresh water stream. Various species of
worms, molluscs, small crustaceans and microorganisms
bury themselves in the mud on the bottom where
conditions are less changeable. They can hide deeper or
close their shells tightly when the salinity becomes
unbearable. These are the exceptions, though, instances of
organisms that have adapted to take advantage of the
resources in an environment that is essentially hostile.

Were the salinity of water anything other than fairly
constant, life would be difficult and perhaps impossible. So
far as living things are concerned its constancy is of great
importance. Happily, it does remain remarkably constant
and has done throughout the whole of history. True, when
an ice age traps water in ice sheets the salinity of the
oceans increases, and when the ice sheets melt and return
their fresh water to the oceans salinity decreases, and no
doubt this causes some problems, but the change is smaller
than you might think and the problems are local. During
the last ice age, for example, the salinity of the Red Sea
increased to around 50 per mille, about 10 per mille more
saline than it is today and high enough to kill most of the
organisms in the Sea.

At present only 3 per cent of the world's water is fresh
water, and 98 per cent of that forms the polar icecaps and

glaciers. Were the whole of that ice to melt, fresh water would flow into the oceans, but as a layer of fresh water floating above the denser salt water. It would take many years for it to mix thoroughly with the sea water and for ocean salinity to alter, and even then the change would amount to less than the 3 per cent you might expect. The volume of the oceans would increase, sea levels would rise, many areas of coastal land would be flooded, and the total surface area of water would increase, probably by more than 3 per cent since the newly flooded areas would form broad but shallow extensions to the oceans. The increased surface area would allow more water to evaporate, and evaporation would tend to increase salinity again. The amount of water in the atmosphere, as vapour or cloud, would increase.

There is another way, too which would compensate for the reduction in salinity as well as any increase in salinity due to a major extension of the ice caps. I shall describe this in a moment.

WHY ISN'T THE SEA SALTIER?

The puzzle is why the sea is not very much saltier than it is. The salts themselves originate in rocks and they are highly soluble in water. As water drains through the land and into rivers it accumulates salts, and the rivers carry them to the sea. This process has continued ever since the oceans and dry land were formed. The salts move from land to sea, but when water evaporates the salts are left behind. Apart from salt crystals that form when water evaporates from droplets of sea spray, it is only the water itself that enters the air, not the salt. That is why it is possible to obtain salt by evaporating sea water, and to obtain fresh water the same way, by condensing the vapour.

It is a fact of life that sometimes causes the serious problem of salination. When land is irrigated by applying fresh water at the surface, it is essential to install efficient drainage to remove the water once it has percolated downwards. If drainage is inadequate the soil becomes wetter. Water then evaporates from the surface and this draws more water upwards through channels among the tiny spaces between soil particles. The water dissolves salts from the soil and from the rock beneath, but only fresh water evaporates at the surface, and so the salts accumulate in the upper layers of the soil. Eventually the region of the soil in which crops grow can become so saline that the plants die. The hotter and drier the climate, the higher the rate of surface evaporation, and so the more rapidly salination occurs.

You can demonstrate this effect easily. Place a salt solution in a jar with a lid, make a hole in the lid just big enough to pass a piece of lamp wick through it, immerse one end of the wick in the liquid, leave a good length exposed to the air, and wait. After a time you will find the jar empty and the wick very salty. The same mechanism explains the extreme saltiness of the Great Salt Lake and the Dead Sea. Salts are carried in by rivers but water is lost mainly by evaporation from the surface. There is nowhere for the salts to go, so they stay where they are and what should be fresh water turns into brine.

The oceans, too, are subject to this process. For more than 4 thousand million years rivers have been washing salts into them. Water can leave the oceans only by evaporation. Therefore, the salts should have been accumulating. After all, there is nowhere for them to go. The seas should have been growing steadily saltier all the time and by now they should be very salty indeed. The water should be so dense you could lie on it without sinking, and probably sit cross-legged on it. You might even be able to walk on it, perhaps by wearing boards, like snow shoes, to distribute your weight over a larger area. Except, of course, that if all the seas were as salty as that life could not have survived for long, so you and I and other would-be marine backpackers would not exist.

WHERE DOES THE SALT GO?

We do exist, we sink whenever we try to sit on top of the sea, and so the salt cannot have accumulated. Something must be removing it as fast as it arrives.

All the great oceans have backwaters, small seas, much shallower than the oceans themselves and often almost totally enclosed by land. The Mediterranean, for example, is linked to its parent, the Atlantic, only at the Strait of Gibraltar. The Adriatic and Aegean Seas form part of the Mediterranean complex but are almost enclosed by land. Only the Dardanelles and Bosporus link the Aegean to the Black Sea and a similarly narrow strait joins the Sea of Azov to the Black Sea. The Mediterranean is the most famous example of what the United Nations calls a regional sea, but there are many smaller ones.

Should the strait linking one of these small seas to its parent ocean become blocked the sea will be isolated. In most cases its level will rise as water continues to drain into it and either the blockage will be breached or a new strait will form, and the link will be re-established. But there are exceptions.

If the rate of surface evaporation is very high, and that implies a warm climate in a low latitude, a point may be reached where the strait feeds water from the ocean into the sea rather than draining it, the water in the sea being lost almost wholly through evaporation. Between this point and that at which the sea is totally sealed, water will enter and evaporate, so the salinity of the enclosed water will increase, at the same time reducing that of the open ocean through the removal of salt. The blocked strait cannot be unblocked by the pressure of rising water because the water level does not rise, it falls. Gradually the sea evaporates and its salts are left behind. Such evaporite deposits are very common and very valuable commercially. We obtain our industrial phosphorus and phosphate-based fertilisers from evaporite deposits of rock phosphate, and supermarket salt comes from mining evaporite deposits of halite, or rock salt.

So salt is removed from the oceans by the evaporation of the water from small, landlocked seas and the regulation is quite subtle. I mentioned earlier that the formation and melting of ice caps does not lead to large changes in ocean salinity, and now you can see why. If ice caps form, removing fresh water from the oceans and therefore tending to increase salinity, sea levels fall. This isolates more of the small seas, whose waters evaporate, thus removing salt. If the ice caps melt, sea levels rise, some of those ancient seas are reflooded, their salt is dissolved, and salt is added to the oceans. Rivers flow, ice ages come and go, and ocean salinity stays the same all the time.

This is the traditional explanation, and so far as living beings are concerned it is very convenient. Perhaps it is a little too convenient, too much of a coincidence that the regulation is so precisely what living cells require. Is anything else happening?

ANIMALS THAT BUILD WALLS

It may be. The organisms themselves may be taking a hand in all this regulation. Think of the two conditions that must be fulfilled for a small sea to become enclosed and then to evaporate. In the first place it must be in a part of the world where the evaporation rate is high; in other words the climate must be warm and dry. Were it not, water would flow into the sea faster than evaporation could remove it. The second condition is that an area of shallow sea must be isolated from the larger water mass; without this isolation water will flow into it, preventing any lowering in its level. Such sea areas do occur in suitably low latitudes, but can they be relied on to be available when they are needed? And how do they become cut off from the larger sea? What is needed is some way of building sea walls. And there are two, reefs and sediments.

Coral reefs can make very effective sea walls. Reefs are built by polyps, very small, soft-bodied animals that protect themselves by secreting calcium carbonate to make a solid base and an outer casing. The polyp lives inside its tube, obtaining food with its tentacles through the open end, and adding to the floor of the tube when it needs to reach a bit further. Not all species of coral polyps live in colonies, but many do, neighbouring tubes joined together to form a solid mass. These are the stony corals (the scientific name is Sceleractinia) and there are about 1,000 species of them.

The polyps do not live alone though. A living reef is a large and complex community. The outer surface of the solid, rock-like material is covered with microorganisms called zooxanthellae, which have some of the characteristics of simple plants but in some ways are like animals. They photosynthesise, using sunlight and taking carbon dioxide from the polyps, and they also take other nutrients from their hosts. During the day the zooxanthellae grow and produce sugars and the polyps build their tubes. At night the polyps feed, using their stinging tentacles to catch anything within reach, up to the size of small fishes. The daily growth of the solid structure forms rings, like the growth rings in trees, and there are also seasonal variations marking the years. These can be read in fossil corals, and have been used to establish the fact that 300 million years ago the Earth took longer to orbit the Sun and there were nearly 400 days in the year.

Because they photosynthesise, the zooxanthellae need sunlight. This means they can inhabit only those places where sunlight penetrates. Some occur in temperate waters, but the great majority are found in clear, tropical waters at depths of between about 15 and 150 feet. They cannot live without corals, nor the coral polyps without them, and so that is where reefs form, and they are very sensitive to pollution and especially to anything that reduces the clarity of the water.

The water must also be warm, with an average temperature no lower than 20 °C (68 °F). Coral reefs, then, occur in warm, shallow, clear seas. Although the polyps are small, most being no more than 3 millimetres (about one-tenth of an inch) in diameter, the reefs they build can be very large. The Great Barrier Reef, off the northeast coast of Australia, is more than 1,000 miles long.

There are three main types of reef: barrier reefs, fringing reefs and atolls, which are named according to they way they form. Barrier reefs, such as the Great Barrier Reef, lie approximately parallel to the coast but separate from it. Fringing reefs, the most common form, grow outwards from the coast, but may touch it at various points, trapping water behind them. Atolls form around the rims of submerged volcanic craters, so they are roughly circular, enclosing a lagoon, and smaller reefs, called patch reefs, may develop inside the lagoon. All three main types are capable of closing off areas of sea. Living reefs do not project above the sea surface, of course — if they did the bits above the surface couldn't live — but should the sea level fall they are likely to be exposed and when that happens the water trapped behind them may well evaporate.

If coral polyps can build walls, ordinary sediment, the remains of once-living marine organisms, can accumulate to raise the sea bed. This provides a means of building dams. The water becomes shallower, more extensive, and liable to evaporate should the inflow of ocean water be prevented, as it would be were the sediment to block a narrow strait or inlet.

IT SOUNDS BELIEVABLE, BUT IS IT TRUE?

Is this how living organisms regulate the salinity of the oceans? It should work. Organic debris is formed in the most productive waters, which are not far from shore, and the debris is then carried by currents to places where it settles as a sediment. The accumulation of sediment is a continuous process, repeatedly closing off shallow arms of the sea and allowing evaporation to separate fresh water from the salts. Coral reefs grow in warm, clear, shallow waters. Should an increase in salinity be associated with a fall in sea level, as in an ice age, reef tops will be exposed and sea water impounded. A decrease in salinity can be due only to a major influx of fresh water, as at the end of an ice age. When that happens sea levels rise, flooding evaporite deposits on what were once, and are now once more, sea beds, the salts dissolve and mix with the ocean waters. Salinity is controlled.

It all sounds plausible, but is it true? We cannot know for certain, but probably it is. Halite (rock salt) deposits are often associated with or found very close to limestones, dolomite or shales. Limestones, as I mentioned earlier, consist mainly of calcium carbonate, the stuff from which coral reefs are made. Dolomite is a calcium-magnesium carbonate. Shales originate from mudstones, rich in organic remains.

The evidence may be circumstantial, but it is strong. If we accept it, we must suppose that the salinity of the oceans, whose constancy is essential for marine life, is regulated by marine organisms themselves by way of major feats of engineering. In the process, and quite irrelevantly, those amiable organisms provide fertiliser for our farmers, salt for our supermarkets and, by making it impossible for us to sit or lie on the sea without sinking, markets for inflatables.

6
DERBYSHIRE BORN

These days I live in Cornwall, but I was born in Derbyshire and spent the first few years of my life there, close to the southern end of the Pennines, the range of limestone hills our teachers were fond of calling the backbone of England. There used to be a jingle describing Derbyshire folk:

Derbyshire born and Derbyshire bred,
Strong in the arm and weak in the head.

It cannot be wholly true, for my arms are thin and puny and always have been, but perhaps I left the place too soon. The jingle was not entirely wrong, though, provided you remember it refers to the past and not the present. Derbyshire is one of a number of places in Britain, and for that matter in most countries, where iodine is relatively uncommon. In defence of Derbyshire I should point out that the Great Lakes region of North America and Switzerland are also places where iodine is naturally in short supply and they have similar problems, and for all I know unsympathetic jingles too.

WE NEED IODINE

When you eat food containing iodine (chemical symbol I), the iodine enters the blood, is carried around the body in the bloodstream, and when it reaches the thyroid gland in the neck just below the larynx (Adam's apple) it reacts with an amino acid, tyrosine, to form a hormone, thyroxin $(C_{15}H_{11}I_4NO_4)$. The thyroxin is released into the blood and plays an important part in a whole range of body processes including the general metabolic rate of the body, which is the rate at which food is converted to energy and therefore the efficiency with which temperature is regulated.

It also affects various growth processes, and not only in humans. In amphibians it regulates metamorphosis from tadpole or pollywog to adult; deprive the young of thyroxin and·they never do turn into frogs, toads or salamanders. The axolotl, famous for remaining a juvenile all its life, will metamorphose into an adult, air-breathing salamander if it is given thyroxin. Thyroxin deficiency in humans may also cause goitre, a swelling that occurs when the thyroid gland expands, apparently in its attempts to produce adequate amounts of the hormone from insufficient material.

In young humans, a shortage of thyroxin, usually caused by a shortage of iodine in the diet, inhibits development and can lead to cretinism and to adults whose metabolisms are sluggish. Often they suffer from myxoedema, a condition in which tissues swell just below the skin. So, to return to Derbyshire, children with too little iodine in their diet may grow into adults of low mental capacity and with bodily swellings that make them look big and strong.

There is a radioactive isotope, iodine-131, commonly released in fallout from weapons and in reactor accidents. Because it can concentrate in the thyroid gland, just as the stable isotope (iodine-127) does, people likely to be exposed to large doses of iodine-131 are sometimes given tablets of potassium iodide to supply a dose of stable iodine large enough to saturate the thyroid so it will accept no more iodine and is thus protected from iodine-131. The radioactive isotope has a half-life of only eight days, so although heavy exposure to it is regarded as a serious health risk, the danger soon passes.

The existence of iodine was unknown before the first decade of the last century and it was isolated for the first time as an element in 1815, by J.L. Gay-Lussac. The realisation that it is essential to our health came much later. We need very little of it. The body of an adult contains between 20 and 50 milligrams of iodine (50 milligrams is about 1.7 thousandths of an ounce) and about 8 milligrams of that are contained in the thyroid, so it is hardly surprising that it took so long to find it. Which foods contain it? The richest source is cod, followed by oysters, halibut and salmon. In a word, it comes mainly from the sea. Most vegetables, meat and dairy products contain very little, but then we need very little.

These days iodine is often added to salt to take care of the needs of people whose food contains less iodine than their bodies require, so the problems of the 'Derbyshire born' are banished to the past and will remain there unless the current fashion for salt-free diets brings back the goitre.

WHY DON'T WE RUN OUT OF IODINE?

It is my Gaian curiosity that leads me to wonder why the situation is not a great deal worse in the matter of iodine. Clearly, iodine originates in the rocks, like most chemical elements, and equally clearly there is not a great deal of it. Sea food and sea fish contain it, and so does sea water, where there is about one part of iodine to every 8,000 parts of chlorine. The iodine must have reached the sea the same way as salt does, by being washed there in rivers. Rivers have been flowing for more than 4 billion years, so by this time you would think the land would have lost so much of its iodine that there would be no possibility of animals finding enough to meet their needs. All of us should have had gross deformities of the thyroid, until they took to adding iodine to our salt; or, more probably, we would have evolved to make much more efficient use of the tiny amounts available to us. One way or another the lack of iodine should have been a much more severe problem than it is, and not only for us. Consider the unfortunate amphibians, doomed, you might think, to perpetual pollywoghood.

Frogs, toads, even most salamanders, grow up, most humans have thyroids that work properly, and so there has to be some means whereby iodine is transported from the sea back to the land. The iodine in supermarket salt is obtained commercially from two principal sources. Chile saltpetre, essentially sodium nitrate ($NaNO_3$), contains small amounts of sodium iodate ($NaIO_3$), extracted as a byproduct during the processing of the nitrate, which is used mainly for fertiliser. Chile saltpetre is an evaporite mineral, formed when the water evaporated from an enclosed arm of the sea. So we can obtain our iodine the way we obtain our salt, by mining evaporites. An alternative source, used increasingly nowadays, is seaweed, processed to extract several of the minerals in which it is rich, including iodine. Iodine is also produced as a byproduct of oil refining. In all cases we take iodine from the sea, because even petroleum was once marine.

These sources work for us, but for most of history there were no human miners or chemical factories, so there has to be another way for iodine to get back to the land without human help. And there is. The seaweeds that concentrate iodine so usefully also release it, as methyl iodide (CH_3I), and in very large amounts. The methyl iodide enters the air as a gas. Most of it reacts with chlorine from sea salt to form methyl chloride (CH_3Cl), the iodine oxidising and the soluble oxide returning to the sea, but some is left in the air, to be carried back over the land where it dissolves in rain water and falls to the ground.

Botanically, the seaweeds are algae, among the simplest and most ancient of all plants, despite the large size to which some of them grow. For all these millions of years they have played a crucial role in moving iodine from the sea back to the land. Were they to disappear, or were we to kill a substantial proportion of them, life on land would become much more difficult. We could rely on the Chile saltpetre mines, but more heavily because before long we would find ourselves having to supply the iodine needs of the land plants and all the other land animals.

RISKS OF RECYCLING

Every so often it happens that a mistake appears in a book that is destined to become a standard textbook. The mistake enters honestly, being the best guess or genuine opinion of the original author, but once installed it can expect a long life, for removing it is exceedingly difficult. The mistake is picked up and repeated by author after author until everyone accepts it as the truth and those who dare to challenge it are not very popular.

I was put in mind of this by two instances that affected me directly, both of them to do with trees. Most reference books tell me that holly rarely grows from its own seed in Britain and that *Aesculus hippocastanum*, the horse chestnut or buckeye chestnut, is alien to Britain and grows only where it is planted, never from its own self-sown seed. I was about to repeat, dutifully, the snippet of information about holly when I noticed a holly tree growing in my own garden in a place where it can have originated only from the germination of a holly seed. In the case of the horse chestnut, I pass two fine specimens on one of my favourite walks and often admire them. One day I was more attentive than usual, and some distance from either adult tree and on the other side of the path I found a young horse chestnut, now about waist high, growing, presumably, from a germinated seed, a conker. The moral, of course, is to do your best to check information before you repeat it, no matter how authoritative its source may seem.

In his search for ways in which important chemical substances are moved from place to place by living organisms, Jim Lovelock came across a mistake of this kind. It concerns the element sulphur.

THE SULPHUR CYCLE

Proteins are made from assemblages of amino acids. There are about 20 amino acids that occur in proteins. Two of them, cysteine and methionine, (as well as cystine which is formed from two molecules of cysteine), contain sulphur, and so sulphur is found in many proteins. This means sulphur is found in all our body tissues. It is also a constituent of thiamin (vitamin B1) and various enzymes, the substances whose presence initiates many important biochemical reactions. Sulphur, then, is an essential nutrient element, and in the first instance it is plants that need it because we obtain all our food, of all kinds, from plants or from animals that eat plants.

The world is not short of sulphur. It is very common, but most of it lies deep below the surface. It is released by volcanoes and is a very common ingredient of minerals. Pyrite is iron sulphide, for example, and galena, an important ore of lead, is lead sulphide. Industrially, we obtain most of the sulphur we use as a byproduct of the refining of sulphide ores and the desulphurisation of coal, natural gas (sour gas) and oil, mainly to reduce pollution by the sulphur dioxide (SO_2) released when sulphur-containing fuels are burned.

Sulphur originates in rocks, and plant roots take it up in the form of sulphate (SO_4) ions carried in solution in the water that moves through the soil. As with so many soluble constituents of living things, sulphate tends to drain to the sea, so we need to find some way for it to return to the land.

This need became apparent in the 1940s, when scientists calculated the amount of sulphur draining into the sea from the land, calculated the rate at which sulphur in surface rocks was being converted into soluble sulphate, and found that about three times more sulphur was entering the sea than the rocks were supplying. Obviously, sulphur was moving from the sea back to the land, but how was it getting back? In order to move from land to sea, rivers provided the means of transport, but the sulphur could move in the opposite direction only through the air.

At some time or other you must have found yourself beside stagnant water, or marshy ground, or have stirred up the sediment on the bottom of a pond, and smelled the hydrogen sulphide bubbling from it. They used to describe hydrogen sulphide as smelling like rotten eggs. It does, but these days the stores supply us with fresh eggs and it may be a long time since you encountered a rotten egg, so the description may be less helpful than it used to be. When the wastes or remains of organisms are left to decompose, various microorganisms convert the sulphur compounds they contain to sulphides, including hydrogen sulphide (H_2S). Other groups of bacteria can use hydrogen sulphide in a version of photosynthesis that involves the sulphide (H_2S) instead of water (H_2O), releasing sulphur rather than oxygen. Then another group oxidises either sulphur or the sulphide, producing sulphate that can be taken up by plants once more.

If oxygen is excluded from the environment, however, oxidation cannot occur and so sulphides accumulate. Most of them react with mineral substances to form stable compounds which then accumulate in the sediment. Sediments may be converted eventually into sedimentary rocks, and there is four times more sulphur in sedimentary rocks than there is in the Earth's crust as a whole. It is concentrated there.

The non-mineralised sulphide includes hydrogen sulphide and when you stir the mud, up it comes to make you pull a face and turn away in disgust. Once hydrogen sulphide enters the air, plenty of oxygen is available to oxidise it to sulphate which dissolves in atmospheric water and makes the rain slightly acid. All natural rainfall is slightly acid.

There is no doubt that it is as dissolved sulphate (dilute sulphuric acid) that the sulphur returns to the land. Nor is there any doubt that the sulphur is of biological origin. Factories and power plants emit sulphur dioxide, of course, and for many years they supplied so much sulphur that there was no need to manufacture sulphur-based fertilisers for farm crops; the rain brought the plants all the sulphur they needed. As with carbon, however, there are light and heavy isotopes of sulphur, and the biological processes are selective. Analyse the sulphate and you can tell whether it came from a human or non-human factory.

Put all this together and the cycle seems to be complete. Sulphate drains into swamps, marshes, estuaries and the sea, enters biological processes, and when marine organisms die it finds its way into the mud, from which oxygen is excluded. Bacteria reduce the sulphur compounds to sulphides and some hydrogen sulphide escapes to the air, is oxidised back into sulphate, and returns to the land in the rain. That is the story as it was worked out in the 1950s, and you will still find textbooks that describe it in this way.

There is only one little, jarring feature to this account, and that is the smell of hydrogen sulphide. If this were the main route by which sulphur returned from water to land, clouds of hydrogen sulphide should be hanging over all swamps, marshes, estuaries, and some parts of the sea, because there is an inevitable delay in oxidising it; the process is effective, but not instantaneous. We should be able to smell it. Indeed, large areas should stink abominably. Swamps and marshes should be dreadful places, and dangerous, because hydrogen sulphide is very poisonous in quite small concentrations and also highly inflammable. Yet you hardly ever hear about exploding swamps.

SULPHUR AND THE SEAWEED

Nevertheless, this is the story the textbooks told, and I dare say some of them still do. Hydrogen sulphide is produced in muds, of course, and some of it does contribute to the return of sulphur from the sea to the land, but this is not the main route. Much more comes from a chemical compound that is made in factories and has some industrial uses but that surprised scientists when it was found to occur naturally. The discovery was made long after the original theory was compiled and the substance is not produced in mud at all.

Probably it all began with plants that had to cope with changes in salinity. *Polysiphonia* is a red seaweed that grows on rocks or on top of other seaweeds. Like most red seaweeds you find it just below the low tide line. At very low tides it may sometimes be exposed. It lives in very shallow water and at low tide it may be temporarily isolated from the sea in rock pools. Water evaporates from the pool, concentrating the salts, and the osmotic pressure increases. There is a range of chemical substances that can help reduce desiccation, and cells containing one such chemical would be able to withstand higher osmotic pressures. It could make survival possible in the hostile environment of a salty tidal pool.

In 1958, F. Challenger reported finding that 15 per cent of the dry weight of *Polysiphonia* consisted of one of these substances, a chemical with the forbidding name dimethylsulphonium propionate, or DMSP. DMSP is released by the seaweed into the water, where it breaks down to yield a simpler substance, DMS (dimethyl sulphide, $(CH_3)_2S$). The DMS enters the air, where it takes part in further reactions that eventually produce microscopically small sulphate particles, on to which water vapour condenses.

Later it was discovered that *Polysiphonia* is not unique. Most of the single-celled plants that float near the surface of the open oceans, the phytoplankton, release DMS. Whether they produce it in response to salt stress or for some other reason is uncertain. What we do know is that they emit quantities of dimethyl sulphide that are sufficient to account for the missing sulphur, the difference between the amount lost from the land and the amount being released from rocks and recycled by other known routes. You could say that we exist by courtesy of the plankton.

The plankton, and their DMS, also exert a strong influence on the world's climates, and the sulphur they return to the land is a principal cause of acid rain, just as the methyl chloride derived from the methyl iodide also released by marine plants is a major source of the chlorine that is involved in the chemistry of the ozone layer. These are matters to which I shall return.

THE LAW OF THE MINIMUM

Some ideas are so familiar to us it is easy to imagine they have been around since antiquity. We know farmers and gardeners feed plants with fertiliser, for example. It seems such an obvious thing to do it can come as something of a surprise to learn that the underlying theory was unknown a century and a half ago. People believed that humus in the soil supplied plants with the food they needed, as food, much like the meals we eat. It was not until 1840, when the German chemist Justus von Liebig published *Die organische Chemie in ihrer Anwendung auf Agrikulturchemie und Physiologie* (The Application of Organic Chemistry to Agricultural Chemistry and Physiology), that this view was challenged.

Von Liebig showed that plants obtained some of their 'food' from air and water and that the nutritional needs of plants and animals could be described in simple chemical terms. He listed the main nutritional requirements and also propounded a law of the minimum. This states that no matter how abundant most nutrients may be, the growth of plants will cease if any one of the required nutrients is missing and that growth, and therefore crop yields, will be restricted by the availability of the scarcest nutrient.

Analyse any plant or animal and you find it consists mainly of carbon, hydrogen and oxygen. These are the elements von Liebig discovered come from air and water. In addition to these, plants require nitrogen, potassium, calcium, phosphorus, magnesium and sulphur. These are called major nutrients because they are needed in relatively large amounts. Each acre of farm crops takes up about 13 pounds (6 kg) each of phosphorus and magnesium, 27 (12 kg) of sulphur, 45 (20 kg) of calcium, and 90 (41 kg) each of nitrogen and potassium. Then there are the minor nutrients, required in much smaller amounts. An acre of crops takes up about one-thousandth of an ounce (30 mg) of cobalt, one-hundredth of an ounce (300 mg) of molybdenum, one-tenth of an ounce (3 g) of copper, one-fifth of an ounce (6 g) each of boron and zinc, and half an ounce (15 g) each of manganese and iron. Plants also require chlorine and some require sodium. Animals also need iodine and selenium.

Fertilisers are nutrients that farmers add to boost the amounts available to plants naturally, and because they are what we can see we may be tempted to think the plants would starve were it not for the attentions of the farmers. They would not, of course, any more than wild plants and animals starve, because despite the vast amounts of fertiliser in use, most nutrients are still supplied without any human intervention at all. Yields would be lower without the use of fertilisers, although organic growers might dispute even this, but the crops would not die, and wild plants have much more modest requirements than cultivated plants which have been bred to concentrate nutrients in their leaves or seeds because they are meant to be eaten.

NUTRIENT CYCLES

The nutrients have to be recycled, used over and over again. When I outlined the way the atmosphere acquired its present composition I described the way nitrogen is supplied by microorganisms. Carbon, too, is cycled by microorganisms that decompose organic remains and return the carbon to the air as carbon dioxide. Chlorine falls in the rain. Some is derived from the salt in sea spray, some is released by volcanoes, but much more enters the air as methyl chloride, released by marine plants. Sulphur and iodine, too, are returned to the land from the sea with the help of those plants, and rain also contains significant amounts of potassium, calcium, magnesium and sodium, and smaller traces of phosphorus. Are they, too, being recycled by living organisms? They may well be.

The results of Hungarian research (by István Dévai, Lajos Felföldy, Ilona Wittner and Sándor Plósz) published in *Nature* in May 1988, threw new light on the way phosphorus is cycled. The scientists studied sewage treatment plants that are exposed to the air and found that nearly half of the phosphorus entering the plant in the sewage was disappearing. It turned out that bacteria in the sediment were converting the phosphorus into phosphine, or phosphorus hydride (PH_3). Phosphine is a gas and that is the form in which the phosphorus enters the air, to be carried back to the land from whence it came.

Even water, the source of hydrogen, is cycled by living organisms. Rain falls, rivers flow, water evaporates, and clouds form, but the water cycle is not quite so simple as it sounds. Plants take water from the soil and it evaporates from tiny pores, the stomata, in their leaves. This evaporation creates the pressure (imagine it as a form of suction) that draws more water upwards. The amount being moved in this way from the soil to the air is considerable. A birch tree, with about a quarter of a million leaves, moves about 80 gallons (about 380 litres) of water a day. Multiply this to the dimensions of a forest and it is not surprising that deforestation can lead to major changes in the local climate.

Once water enters the air as vapour it does not necessarily form clouds, even when the air is saturated. For clouds to form, there must be small particles, of just the right size, on to which the vapour can condense. Over land these particles consist mainly of soil grains, but over the oceans there is no dust. There the particles consist mainly of sulphate and the sulphate is derived from DMS, the substance emitted by the phytoplankton and the route by which so much sulphur is returned to the land.

MICROBIAL METALLURGISTS

Carbon, hydrogen, oxygen, nitrogen, sulphur, iodine and now phosphorus make up an impressive list containing most of the substances needed by living things, and in years to come further discoveries are likely to be added to it. These essential nutrients flow down to the sea and are returned, pushed back up the hill as it were, by living organisms.

Nor does the process end there. We humans have taken to mining the rocks for their minerals and we have living organisms to thank for some of those minerals. Carbonate minerals, those containing 'locked away' carbon dioxide and found in rocks such as limestones, are biological in origin, and so are many sulphides found in sedimentary rocks.

We even employ microorganisms to obtain certain metals that are valuable but inaccessible or dispersed very thinly. Some bacteria concentrate particular metals naturally, others have to be genetically engineered to make them do it or do it better, but the process works. The bacteria need the substances with which the metals are compounded, are able to take what they need, and the metals are their waste product. Water containing a bacterial culture is sprayed on to the rock, the particular metal is concentrated by the bacteria and then extracted from the water draining from the site. Copper, manganese and uranium are just three of the metals that have been obtained this way, and bacteria have been used to obtain pure sulphur from the evaporite mineral gypsum.

Suddenly our mental image of the world shifts, though in emphasis more than substance. There is nothing new in describing what are known technically as the biogeochemical cycles of elements. Scientists have known for many years that the elements I have listed are involved in biological processes, for part of the time are recycled from dead organic matter back to living organisms through the processes of decomposition, and that little by little they are carried away in water, eventually to the oceans. The conventional view is that ordinary chemistry and physics dominate the cycle from that point until the one at which the elements are taken up once more by plants. This is the emphasis that is changing, for it appears that what were thought to be non-biological parts of the cycle in fact are driven biologically.

If the air, the oceans, even many of the rocks themselves are in some sense being manipulated directly by the mass of living beings, we have little choice but to abandon the old view of the way the world works and struggle to find a new one. The new one is what Lovelock called Gaia.

7
THE SUM OF ITS PARTS

Back in school, I expect the story they told you about life on Earth was much like the one they told me. The teacher explained that the Earth formed, along with the rest of the solar system, and was uniquely fortunate because of its position in relation to the Sun. This position meant that, as soon as the planet had settled down, conditions on it were favourable for life. Venus, similar to Earth in so many ways, was just that bit too close to the Sun and so it was too hot for anything to live on it. Mars was just that bit too far away, so it never became warm enough, although there was just a possibility that some kind of life existed there.

From the time life appeared on Earth conditions have remained hospitable. The climate has never been too extreme and although there have been ice ages there has never been a time when the entire planet froze. Nor has it ever been too hot. The original atmosphere contained enough carbon dioxide to make photosynthesis possible, so green plants evolved. They supplied the oxygen that to this day makes life possible for air-breathing species, including ourselves.

The teacher went on to explain that it took a long time for life to appear and when it did there followed another long period during which it evolved very slowly and nothing much appeared to be happening. Then, around 600 million years ago, all the major groups of animals appeared, pretty well all at once. After that things happened fast and it was not long before the pattern was set for all the relatively minor evolutionary adjustments that have occurred since.

These adjustments are modifications in plants and

animals that take place in response to local environmental conditions and changes, over which plants and animals exert no influence whatever. The changes themselves may be challenges or opportunities. Often they are both. When the air came to contain oxygen, animals evolved to breathe it. When the weather grew cold or hot, wet or dry, species either adapted to the changes, moved to pleasanter climes, or became extinct.

ONE WORLD OR TWO?

The overall impression is of a world you can think of as divided into two parts. There is a physical and chemical part, and a separate biological part. The physical and chemical part consists of the air, the oceans, the rocks, the climate, and most of the constitutents of what we can sum up as the environment. It is vast, inanimate, pre-existing and governed wholly by the laws of chemistry and physics. So far as living things are concerned it is the given, that which is there at the start and through all eternity. Plants and animals adapt to the conditions it provides, consume the foods it provides, and if it changes they roll with the punches or are destroyed. In its inanimate way it influences them, indeed in some sense controls their destinies, but there is no way they can alter it. They are just passengers.

Naturally, living things have relationships among themselves. Animals eat plants, and one another, for example, and parasites have hosts, so in addition to adapting to the given conditions, species have to take account of the living things around them. Evolutionary adaptation must respond to this second, and secondary, living aspect of the environment at the same time as it equips species to cope with the basic physical and chemical conditions around them. Gazelles have to be able to see lions and outrun them, many plants have thorns to deter grazers, and many animals have cunning disguises to help them hide from predators or to make them closely

resemble other, quite unrelated species that have more
formidable defences.

Humans have a special place in the scheme of things,
because plants and animals can be arranged
hierarchically. Some are 'lower', others 'higher'. The
ranking is not moralistic but based on a logical evaluation
of features. It is rational, objective, and it is pure
coincidence that you and I find ourselves sitting on the top
of the heap. Our position on the top of the heap gives us
certain powers and accompanying responsibilities. In
particular, humans and only humans are capable of
altering the chemical and physical conditions for existence.
We can do nothing so blasphemous as suppose we might
improve the world, but we can most assuredly wreck it and
wipe out all life.

THE THEOLOGY OF SPACESHIP EARTH

If this description sounds extreme or crude, remember the
environmentalist interpretations that were placed on the
first photographs of Earth taken from space. Spaceship
Earth the planet was called. Its image appeared
everywhere, and still does — blue and green, with curling
wisps of white cloud, bathed in its own gentle luminescence
as though smiling at its benign parent, the Sun. It is
hospitable, welcoming, and quite alone in the vastness of a
universe so hostile that a being removed from Earth must
die instantly. It is the vehicle on which we ride. We are
sometimes called the crew because, although we play no
part in guiding the ship or deciding its destination, we have
the power to destroy it. The word 'crew' seems curiously
inappropriate. If the environmentalist warnings are to be
taken seriously we are more like unruly delinquents who
have escaped from captivity.

Or perhaps, in this scenario, we really are a crew, but a
rebellious, mutinous one, defying the orders of a captain in
whose judgment we have lost faith. In *The Night of the
Iguana* Tennessee Williams described our relationship with
the natural environment as 'man's inhumanity to God'. Is

this what the environmental movement is really saying? Is this the story, retold in modern language, of *Paradise Lost*? Did God create the world not from nothing but from His own substance, as Milton believed, making the Earth itself sacred, its materials as well as its divine origin? Is our desire to liberate ourselves from the constraints imposed by our environment, to dominate nature, albeit with great courage and intellectual brilliance, no more than egotism, the arrogant defiance of Satan? As individuals, are we tempted through our vanity and desire for knowledge, like Adam and Eve, so that mankind as a whole, mainly through its science and technology, has come to represent Satan, individual men and women the occupants of the Garden? If such a comparison can be drawn it is small wonder the Spaceship Earth image (the Garden) and the environmentalist critique resonated so powerfully throughout Western cultures. The indictment was, quite literally, damning, and the only sentence likely on conviction was not extinction and painless oblivion but eternal torment. Nor is it surprising that environmental concern developed more slowly in regions with a different cultural heritage.

DARWINISM

Back in school, though, I was being taught science, not theology, and the rise of environmental awareness was still 20 years in the future. So far as it described the origin of the Earth, the science was based on as much as the teacher had heard about the current state of geological knowledge. When it described the evolution of species it was based on Darwinism.

The idea of evolution was not conceived by Charles Darwin. By the time he embarked for his famous voyage on HMS *Beagle* many scientists accepted that the species of plants and animals we see around us developed from earlier species. Darwin's contribution was to draw together a large body of observations, deduce an explanatory theory to link them, and then to reduce that theory to a series of propositions.

In its simplest formulation the theory is very elegant. Darwin observed that within any species parents produce, or are capable of producing, a larger number of offspring than the two required to replace them, so populations tend to increase. Populations cannot increase indefinitely because a point will be reached beyond which the resources, such as food and shelter, will be insufficient to sustain all those needing them. Therefore offspring will compete for the limited resources. The successful will be those that find food, shelter and mates, and thus they will produce more offspring than their less successful rivals to form the next generation.

The difference between successful and unsuccessful individuals must consist in small variations of physique or behaviour. These variations appear at random and are inherited by offspring from their parents, so they are transmitted from each generation to the next. Therefore advantageous variations will tend to accumulate, disadvantageous ones to disappear because individuals possessing them have fewer offspring, and little by little the characteristics of the species will change, with new variations constantly appearing and being tested against the environment.

From time to time the accumulated changes will be such as to distinguish certain members of a species living in one area or in particular ways from other members, so that members of this group no longer interbreed with members of other groups and what was one species has become two. Darwin's finches provide the classic example of such speciation. These are birds, found only in the Galápagos Islands, that must have descended from a single, mainland species whose descendants adapted to different diets, evolved bills appropriate to the foods they ate, and in time became 14 distinct species.

Darwinism and the more modern neo-Darwinism which extends Darwin's work to embrace genetics and most aspects of ecology (the study of relationships among communities of organisms and between communities and their inanimate environment) are concerned with the evolution of species. The concept of Gaia, of the totality of all species acting together like a single organism, does not conflict with this accepted view. It does not question the mechanisms by which evolution occurs. It does, however, challenge the Spaceship Earth view of the planet and any suggestion that the inhabitants of our world are passengers, being carried by a vehicle over which they have no control or, in the case of humans, only a potential for harm.

IS EARTH UNIQUE?

The story I was told at school begins well enough, with the formation of a solar system that included a lifeless Earth. The first mistake lies in the assumption that our position within the solar system in uniquely favourable for the development of life. It may be and, since our close neighbours Venus and Mars are lifeless, perhaps it is, but we should not assume it is necessarily so.

My teacher imagined a very long period, of billions of years, before life appeared. Had there been such a period the argument for the uniqueness of our position would have some substance. Three planets lay ready and waiting but after a long time life appeared on only one of them, suggesting the other two were unsuitable. We know now, though, that this is not what happened. There was no long waiting period. Life existed on Earth within 800 million years of its formation and had probably existed for quite some time before that. When you allow for the turmoil of continuing bombardment from lumps of rock as the accretionary phase of planetary formation approached its end, and the violence of volcanic activity on the newly formed planet, it is no exaggeration to say that life appeared just as soon as the place settled down sufficiently to permit it. At that stage it might also have appeared on Venus or Mars or both of them. So far as we can tell it did not, but this may be nothing more than chance. Certainly it cannot have been due to the distance of any of these three planets from the Sun, whose radiation made one too hot and the other too cold, for at that time solar radiation was very much weaker than it is now. Venus cannot have been too hot, and Earth was rather cold.

Once that phase passed, however, and life appeared, conditions might have taken an alarming turn. The carbon dioxide in the atmospheres of Earth and Venus exerted its greenhouse warming effect, conserving the weak radiation from the Sun, but as the Sun grew hotter climates might have become dangerously hot. On Earth, as we know, carbon was being removed from the atmosphere on a large scale more than 3,500 million years ago, and such major activity implies not just life but a great deal of life. Had living organisms been few in number and localised in a few places, carbon removal could not have proceeded rapidly enough and such life as there was would have been destroyed. Planets cannot support 'just a little bit of life' for very long. It has to be a lot, or none at all.

Once they are present it is easy to see how single-celled organisms can proliferate rapidly. Bacteria reproduce by cell division, one cell becoming two. Under favourable conditions they can divide in this way every 20 minutes, a rate at which it takes less than seven hours for one cell to multiply to a million.

It is possible, then, that life made attempts on Venus and Mars, but started slowly and failed. We know both planets are now lifeless, but the expeditions planned for Mars in the 1990s will search for signs of past life, so perhaps that question will be answered.

PASSENGERS OR CREW?

As we have seen, the burial of carbon, the transformation of the chemical composition of the atmosphere and its subsequent maintenance as a constant but inherently unstable mixture of gases, and thus the regulation of the long-term climate, was but the beginning. The composition of the oceans is also manipulated, the chemical ingredients needed by living organisms of all kinds are transported to where they are needed, and possibly harmful ingredients are removed.

It is no longer possible to believe that the chemical and physical environment lies beyond any possibility of influence by living beings. We are compelled to abandon the Spaceship Earth picture of an essentially inanimate vehicle that, by our greatest good fortune, just happens to be habitable. Living organisms as a whole are not passengers. They are crew, operating the ship (if not steering it), but they are more than that. It was they who built the ship's 'life-support system' and set it working immediately after the ship was launched. It is truly their ship, and habitable because they have made it so.

This means we must also abandon the notion that we humans are unique in our ability to alter the world around us. All living things do this.

THE FACE OF THE EARTH

There is yet more, or at least there may be, derived from things that were not even dreamt of in my old teacher's philosophy. What could he have known of continental drift, sea-floor spreading, and the theory of plate tectonics that unites them?

The idea of continental drift is quite old. At the edges of all continents the land slopes away to a region from which it plunges steeply into the oceanic abyss. Part of this land, the continental shelf, is flooded by the sea. If you look at a map of the world, but especially at one that shows the edges of the continental shelves rather than the present-day coastlines, you can hardly help being struck by the fact that some continents look as though they might fit snugly against others. The fact that particular species of plants and animals can be found on continents now widely separated by the sea reinforces the idea that certain of the continents were once joined and that, somehow, they have drifted apart. That is continental drift.

In the centre of each of the major oceans there is a

region of submarine mountains and volcanoes. At these regions, the mid-oceanic ridges, new rock is being erupted from below the Earth's crust, spreading out to either side, and then fresh eruptions are breaking through again at the centre. This is forcing the oceans to grow wider. The process is called sea-floor spreading and it is obviously related to continental drift.

If oceans are growing wider in some places they must be growing smaller in others, and to explain and draw together ideas of continental drift and sea-floor spreading a more comprehensive theory of plate tectonics was developed. Tectonic, from the Greek *tektonikos*, simply means pertaining to building or construction.

The theory holds that below the Earth's crust there is a region in which hot and very dense rock behaves like a fluid. Above it the crust of solid rock consists of a number of plates, coherent pieces, some large, others small, that are moved by motions in the underlying material. Where two plates are carried away from each other new crust is formed, but in other places plates are moving past one another, their edges parallel and grinding together, or colliding, one descending below its neighbour. As you may imagine, when two plates made from solid rock collide, things do not proceed smoothly. One does not just glide beneath the other in a continuous motion. It sticks, resists, and then moves in shudders and jerks that cause earthquakes.

Beneath the ocean the edges of plates are coated in sediments rich in the remains of once-living organisms. Do these sediments influence plate motion? Do they facilitate the movement of one plate beneath another, like a lubricant? Do they retard it, acting like a brake? When continents collide, much sedimentary rock is pushed upwards to form mountain chains and the quantity of material involved is vast. The Alps and Himalayas are largely made from such rocks and were formed fairly recently. The raising of the Himalayas is not yet completed; they are still growing higher. Do the sediments make it easier for plates to move in some places than in others? If they do, does their effect add up to an influence on the speed and direction of continental drift? Does the weight of sediment affect the pressure overlying places where the crust is otherwise weak, so influencing volcanic activity?

The formation of mountains (the technical term is orogeny) alters the appearance of the surface of the Earth, but it is much more important than that. It is a truly mighty recycling operation. The weathering and erosion of surface rocks releases minerals. Some are carried away at once by rivers, some are used by plants and animals, delaying their departure, but sooner or later all of them end on the sea bed as sediment. Heated and compressed to form sedimentary rocks, often transformed by further heating or exposure to hot rocks or liquids from below the crust to form metamorphic rocks, twisted, folded, contorted in many ways, some of them may be thrust above the water surface once more. The process of weathering and erosion begins all over again, but the minerals have been returned from the sea bed. They are available again to living organisms. Life can continue.

Does the fact that Earth supports life modify such essentially geophysical processes to this extent? It may do, although with our present knowledge of those processes we can only speculate. We can compare Earth with Venus and Mars, of course. Both these planets have volcanoes, so their interiors are hot and weaknesses in the crust allow material to erupt to the surface. On Earth such volcanically active regions might indicate the margins of plates, but the Martian crust does not appear to be divided into plates, and that of Venus may not be either. We do not know, but the thought that the movement of continents is linked to the presence of life is intriguing.

THE EARTH AS A SYSTEM

We have demolished most of my schoolteacher's cherished notions about the way the Earth works, but no blame is attached to him. He did the best he could with the information he had, and those lessons took place more than 40 years ago. Since his time we have learned much. We know that life appeared on Earth very soon after the planet formed. We know that the Earth is much affected by the life that exists on it and that the effect is fundamental, relating to its essential chemistry and physics rather than being a mere cosmetic, a greening of the surface. We know that, far from being passive in relation to the inanimate environment, living beings manipulate that environment in ways favourable to the continuance of life. We suspect that this manipulation may extend to the large-scale structuring of the Earth's crust. This must influence our view of the way evolution proceeds, involving a further extension of the neo-Darwinist view to encompass the new definition of the relationship between what lives and what does not.

The new image is of a system, and that is how Jim Lovelock regards it. What is a system? In the sense I am using it here, it is an entity, a discrete 'thing', distinguishable from all other 'things', that is able to maintain its own integrity by responding appropriately to changes. Its responses involve the possession of sensors to detect change and links from the sensors to the parts of the system that must react. This conveyance of information about change from a sensor to a part of the system is called feedback and in most cases it works in a negative sense, to restore an equilibrium that might be lost. The governor on a steam engine provides a simple example of a feedback mechanism. Spinning weights are moved outwards or inwards by changes in the speed of the engine, so they are the sensors. An arrangement of levers links the weights to a steam valve that closes if the engine speed increases, spinning the weights outward, and opens if it decreases and the weights move inward. The opening and closing of the valve are the feedback response and the effect is to maintain a constant engine speed.

Seen as a whole, as a discrete entity, the Earth has many 'governors'. The climate is regulated, for example. As the output from the Sun increased, temperatures were held constant by a feedback mechanism. Materials are cycled so that supplies are delivered to places where they sustain organisms. By such means the entity maintains its own integrity, holds constant the conditions under which it exists. We are justified, therefore, in regarding Earth as a single system.

This does not mean, of course, that henceforth we must regard it only in such a holistic way. The system is large and complex, containing within itself innumerable subsystems, and information about these is needed and can be obtained only by studying them separately, as though they were divorced from the total system. If the carburettor fails on a car we take it out and fix it, without pondering too deeply on the rest of the machine, yet we remain well aware that the part has meaning only in the context of the whole machine. It is our perception of the whole that must change.

Entities need names, for convenience if nothing else. Gaia is the name that has been given to the Earth seen as a system, to contrast it with the more usual sense of Earth seen as a planet.

LIVING SYSTEMS

Gaia, then, is a system. The human body is also a system. At least, it can be regarded as such, sometimes usefully. It functions at a constant temperature, for example, and should the internal temperature rise or fall the body sweats or shivers or takes more extreme action to restore its equilibrium. The salinity and acidity of its internal fluids are also held constant, substances being added or removed as required. Necessary fuel and construction materials are transported around the body and any organ that needs them takes them as they pass.

What is true of the human body is equally true of any living being. Think of something that is alive but as far removed from a human as you can imagine. What about a slime mould, a community of amoeba-like cells that now and then join together to make a kind of tower, involved in reproduction, or a thing rather like a tiny slug that moves in search of new sources of food? It does not regulate its internal temperature, but its chemical composition is held constant, so it regulates itself as a system. It is not so different in principle from the human body.

BACK TO THE TWO DOG PROBLEM

Without attempting anything so ambitious as a definition, perhaps this allows us to say a little more about the two dog problem. The question, you may recall, was how may we distinguish that which is alive from that which is not? Might it be that to qualify as being alive an entity must be a self-regulating, self-sustaining system? The living dog is self-sustaining; in the dead dog the system has broken down totally. Its vital functions have ceased, and those functions represent the easily detectable part of its sensory and feedback mechanisms.

In case this sounds too mechanistic, as though I were proposing that living beings are mere machines, I should emphasise my use of the word 'self'. A machine, made by someone, depends on outside help. The steam engine survives only because there is a team of engineers to keep it going and to make sure it does not starve for want of the fuel it is incapable of finding for itself. Living things invariably find their own fuel, and they are their own engineers. They resemble machines, at least in some ways, but they are far from being mere machines.

For internal temperature read climate. For chemical composition read atmospheric composition and ocean salinity. For transport of fuel and construction materials read cycling of elements. The system that is Gaia seems to behave in very much the same way as the systems we recognise as living bodies.

Take what we can say about the distinction between living and non-living matter, relate it to what we know about the way the Gaia system functions, and the conclusion is inescapable. Gaia must be a single, discrete, living organism.

8
RED IN TOOTH AND CLAW?

It begins to sound as though living things, all of them, are bound together in some kind of collaboration. You might almost call it a benign conspiracy. This is something else that would have puzzled my old schoolteacher. Like most people of his generation, and many of our own, he believed nature is 'red in tooth and claw', a battlefield in which each individual is in conflict with all others. You can still find politicians who see the world, and especially human society, this way, but it is a perverse view that owes little to the facts of the case.

The phrase 'red in tooth and claw' is often linked to the name of Charles Darwin, but wrongly. It was not he who coined it but the poet Tennyson, and some years before 1859 when *The Origin of Species* was first published. The words suggest that Tennyson had an idea of evolution and of relationships among species, but the long poem *In Memoriam* in which they occur reveals that Tennyson's view was rather different from Darwin's. The poem was written, over a period of about 17 years, in sadness at the death of Arthur Hallam, a close friend, and it presents humans as the latest and most splendid product of nature's process, struggling to advance toward a perfected state where they will be freed from the brutish struggle in which all other creatures are engaged. For Tennyson, evolution was the working out of God's design and it leads to the completion of human knowledge and perfection of the human spirit. His friend, he says, recognised this.

Who trusted God was love indeed
And love Creation's final law —
Tho' Nature, red in tooth and claw
With ravine, shriek'd against his creed —

It is a religious view of the world, and by no means pessimistic because it predicts a final condition of harmony and freedom, the 'one far-off divine event, To which the whole creation moves'. Along the way Tennyson wrote another line that has become as famous as 'red in tooth and claw':

> Of those that, eye to eye, shall look
> On knowledge; under whose command
> Is Earth and Earth's, and in their hand
> Is Nature like an open book;

We are offered hope, but in a vision that supposes evolution to be directed toward an identifiable goal that was defined from the start. This is determinism, a philosophical or theological view most scientists cannot accept and that, in particular, should not be applied to evolutionary processes, for reasons I shall try to explain in the next chapter, and it is the single feature that most clearly sets Tennyson's interpretation of the process apart from Darwin's.

SURVIVAL OF THE FITTEST

A second phrase no less closely associated with Darwin is 'the survival of the fittest'. This, too, sounds fairly brutal, a prescription not far removed from 'might is right'. Certainly Darwin adopted 'the survival of the fittest'. Indeed he used it in later editions of *The Origin*, but he did not coin it and its use has led to no end of trouble. If the 'fittest' are to survive, how shall we recognise them? Are they the biggest, toughest, most aggressive, in fact the bullies? What are they 'fit' for? To survive? Is that how we can know they are fit — because they survive? The argument begins to sound tautological as well as brutal, but it was not in the least either brutal or tautological as Darwin first expounded it, without the help of this unfortunate catchphrase.

'Survival of the fittest' was coined by Herbert Spencer in an essay he wrote in 1852 called 'A theory of population,

deduced from the general law of animal fertility'. He had
developed an evolutionary theory of his own, but was
concerned more with the evolution of intelligent beings and
human society than with biological evolution in general
and, like so many people of his time, he was a firm believer
in 'progress'. He saw evolution culminating in equilibrium,
when all would be harmony, all conflicts nicely balanced,
and the utilitarian ideal realised, with the greatest good
accruing to the greatest number. Scientifically, of course,
evolution is seen as an unending process in which any idea
of 'progress' is meaningless. Spencer's view has no
scientific support, even though part of it remains
politically important because it gave rise to what in fact is
called social Darwinism but what should be known as
social Spencerism.

Darwin, the gentlest of men, has thus been saddled
posthumously with concepts that were not his and that
lend support to right-wing political creeds of selfishness
and violence that would have appalled him. To be fair, his
name is also used to sanction left-wing ideas of the
perfectibility of people through the provision of an ideal
environment, and he did not say that either, though he
might have found it less offensive.

A BRUTAL WORLD?

Be that as it may, the Gaian idea that all living beings are
engaged in a benign conspiracy of cooperation seems hard
to swallow. We have been brought up on TV wildlife
documentaries, after all, and we have seen it all. We have
watched the lions tearing apart the antelope, the sharks in
a feeding frenzy, the spider assassinating the fly, and the
mantis praying for lunch to stroll within reach. It is a
brutal world, there is no doubt of that, and when the
victims have blood, it is bloody, too. And if you switch
channels to escape you are more than likely to encounter
human brutalities just as terrible. Darwin may have been a
gentle, kind man who would never knowingly harm any
living thing, but the world he helped describe is not a safe

or pleasant place to live, unless you happen to be one of the top bullies.

Or is it? Animals must eat. That is all we have seen them doing and there is another side to the story. Divide all species into two groups, of those that eat and those that are eaten (with most species falling into both groups, of course) and it is clear that the eaters are moderate in their demands. The eaten do not vanish as a group. If they did, the eaters would starve. So there is some mechanism at work preventing the eaters from going too far. The antelope that falls prey to hungry lions dies violently, but one antelope feeds a family of lions and the lions will not hunt again until they are hungry, and not then if they come across an antelope that has died in some other way. Meanwhile, the sisters, brothers, cousins, aunts, sons and daughters of the victim survive. There are far more antelopes than there are, or could possibly be, lions and the relationship between the eaters and the eaten is but one of the vast range of relationships among individuals and species. The TV gives us a dramatic view of things, but one that is misleading. It exaggerates and sensationalises.

Most animals are social, to a greater or lesser extent, and they collaborate among themselves according to sets of rules. The first antelope to spot trouble warns the rest of the herd, at some risk to itself, so all but one can escape. That is their way. When musk oxen see wolves approaching they form a defensive circle, with the young and the weakest in the centre, so the wolves face a wall of sharp and deadly horns. Within a pride, lions help one another and, within a pack, so do wolves. Indeed, it is the broad similarity between the societies of wolves and of humans that made it possible for the wolf to adapt easily to human ways and allowed us to change it into the domestic dog. We can recognise as social the animals that live together in herds, flocks or schools, such as horses, cattle, sheep, as well as many birds and fishes, but social relationships are the rule, not the exception. Most animals are social, or can be when circumstances permit.

Some years ago, in collaboration with Peter Crawford, I wrote a book (*The Curious Cat*) based on a study of farm cats sponsored by the BBC Natural History Unit. The domestic cat is supposed to be one of the most solitary, most antisocial, of all animals. These cats were observed closely for a year, during which time their contact with humans was kept to a minimum. It became clear that their social relationships were complex, and there were surprises. Young cats were put in charge of kittens, to look after and play with them while their mothers hunted or rested, and on one occasion a cat carried food quite a long way and presented it to a mother whose kittens were too young for her to leave them. The sharing of food, except between parents and offspring, marks a high degree of cooperation, especially since in this case the donor's subsequent behaviour revealed it to be very hungry itself.

Such detailed study of animal behaviour did not begin until long after the time of Darwin, Tennyson and Spencer. We should not criticise them for being ignorant of it. Yet it changes our view of the world profoundly. 'Survival of the socially cohesive' lacks the ring of 'survival of the fittest', but it may be more accurate.

ARE ANIMALS AGGRESSIVE?

There is another observation, too, that must modify the moralistic or political aspect of the way we see the world. In the relationship between predators and their prey, it is only while it is hungry and hunting that the predator represents any kind of threat, and the prey know this. A wolf can walk through a herd of caribou and be ignored unless it is hunting, an activity it reveals in its bodily stance and general attitude. Most mammals fear snakes and leave them well alone, but unless they are threatened only hungry snakes are dangerous.

The adder (*Vipera berus*) is Britain's only venomous snake. A friend of mine found a large female adder in his garden and decided to provoke it to see just how aggressive the beast is. He used a stick to prod and poke at it, but it took little notice, so he flipped it over on to its back. It turned itself the right way up again and tried to go back to sleep. Eventually, under extreme provocation, it moved away into the undergrowth for a bit of peace. I have another friend, who, while photographing wildlife in Africa, came across a puff adder near the camp. He photographed it, but otherwise left it undisturbed. It stayed where it was for a fortnight, and people had to step across it to get past, but it took no notice of them.

Few animals, if any, are essentially aggressive. They are not looking for trouble and in most cases conflicts between members of a group are resolved ritually, without inflicting injury. With this realisation the image of a world in which all beings are in a state of perpetual war, each against all, evaporates entirely. The image is just plain wrong. The world is not in the least like that.

This mistaken view of the violence inherent in the natural world arises in part because of a misunderstanding about the meaning of the word 'competition'. It is a word, and concept, derived from economic theory, and in the last century evolutionary, economic and social theories became closely intertwined, but modern biologists have modified its original meaning. Biologically, competition — in Darwin's words, the struggle for life — has little to do with cheating or robbing rivals, although these things happen, and even less to do with individuals seizing for themselves more resources than they need. It is simply that some individuals are more likely than others to reproduce and it is not necessarily the bullies who win.

In times of stress it has been found, from studies of European wood mice for example, that the survivors are individuals closest to the average size. The small individuals need relatively large amounts of food to grow and to maintain their body temperature, but, being smaller and weaker, they are less able to find it. The big bullies, on the other hand, can find food, but they need even larger amounts because of their larger size. Eventually they also succumb. It is not quite the meek that inherit the Earth, but at least it is the ordinary, the average.

INDIVIDUALS OR COMMUNITIES?

This mistaken view of violence in the natural world also partly arises from our habit of studying organisms as individuals, rather than as groups. This is why more recent findings from studies of behaviour and ecology, which consider groups rather than individuals, compel us to revise earlier opinions.

Most of what we know about animals, or about ourselves for that matter, comes from studying individuals under controlled conditions. If you want to know how a body works, how an animal moves and functions, it is difficult to see how else you could find reliable answers. Yet even then, the body of an animal can be regarded as a community, or as the kind of system I discussed in the last chapter, and at several levels. You might consider the contribution each organ and gland makes to the whole organism, for example, conceiving of the body as a system in which each part makes sense only in relation to the whole, the parts served with nutrients and a waste-disposal facility by the blood and lymphatic subsystems and with information and feedback provided by the nervous subsystem. Such a description is fine so far as it goes, but if you need to repair a part of the system you will need to know much more about how that part works. So each part becomes a subsystem in its own right, with its own network of sub-subsystems. The sequence of Chinese boxes is not infinite, though. From the biological point of view the limit is the cell. Each part of the body is a cohesive community of cells performing a defined function.

The body of any animal or plant can be regarded as such a community of cells, but cells, too, are commonly considered in isolation. This is especially true of free-living cells, those living organisms that consist of nothing more than one cell. Here, at the very basis of life, surely we should find individuals that live separate existences, each independent of the others. At this level even reproduction does not demand an encounter between two individuals. Cells simply divide.

Think of bacteria, among the simplest of beings. You can see pictures in textbooks of a bacterium, and it will have a taxonomic name, genus and species in most cases, worked out on the same principles as are applied to plants and animals. It looks like an individual being that goes about its business all by itself, dividing now and then to produce daughters, and taking no notice of its fellows.

This view is just as wrong as the view of animals constantly fighting one another, and for the same reason. Bacteria do not live as isolated individuals. Indeed, in ways that seem strange, almost weird, they may be the most highly social of all organisms, to their great profit.

THE SOCIETY OF THE BACTERIA

A few kinds of bacteria can cause illness in humans and this fact led to the development of antibiotics, drugs that kill bacteria. Antibiotics had been in use for only a few years before strains of bacteria began to appear that were immune to them. This fact was attributed to mutation and natural selection. It was assumed that variation among a particular bacterial population allowed for some individuals that were immune to the drug. They survived, their progeny inherited their immunity, and so an immune strain emerged.

There was a slight problem with this theory, in that when resistance appeared it was often not only to a single antibiotic but to up to six different antibiotics. Resistance occurred all over the world and this, presented a problem. It happened too rapidly, among bacterial strains separated by vast distances, for mutation and natural selection to be a really convincing explanation. Indeed, a bacterium contains so few genes that a mutation, usually involving the loss or disablement of a gene, is almost invariably fatal.

Recent research suggests a partial and startling explanation. It has been found experimentally in cultures of *Escherichia coli*, a common bacterial species, that mutation is not always random. It can also occur in a selective way to provide genes that help the organism adapt quickly to a change in its environment, such as the presence of a poison. This contradicts conventional evolutionary theory, of course, in which mutations occur randomly and are then subjected to natural selection.

It still does not account for the rapid transmission of drug resistance, but there is now an explanation for that, too. The story is recounted, clearly and concisely, by Professor Sorin Sonea in *The Sciences* (July/August 1988). The bacteria acquiring resistance were not mutating, they were exchanging genetic information amongst themselves in the form of tiny fragments, much like viruses, called R plasmids. These replicated independently of the cells they occupied so they migrated from bacterial strain to strain, infecting their hosts with the capacity to resist the drugs.

When a bacterium dies and disintegrates, sections of its genes disperse and under certain circumstances can pass through the cell walls of living bacteria to be incorporated there. Environmental changes can cause certain sections of genetic material within bacteria, called prophages, to start reproducing themselves rapidly and to manufacture protective coverings and tails which act as anchors. At this stage they are called bacteriophages or simply phages. Eventually there are so many of them within a bacterium that the bacterial cell bursts, releasing phages that can survive for long periods, during which time they are dispersed by wind or water until they encounter a suitable bacterial host. Then a phage attaches itself to the cell wall by its tail and injects its genes through the wall.

When a bacterium finds itself in a new environment for which it is ill-equipped, these are ways in which it is able to acquire the genes it needs to help it from other bacteria in its immediate neighbourhood. And how did those bacteria acquire them? Perhaps it was by selective mutation.

It is misleading to think of bacteria as isolated individuals. They exist as local communities, within which different bacteria, usually assigned to distinct species, perform particular tasks. It seems they are able to modify their own genes to suit their circumstances. They can exchange genetic information amongst themselves when environmental conditions dictate, and because of the way they do this, using fragments of material that can survive long periods and travel long distances, local communities communicate with other local communities. The speed with which antibiotic resistance emerged throughout the world suggests strongly that at least some of the time this communication takes place on a global scale.

Such an intimate relationship between each individual and all the others means that the very concept of an individual bacterium requires heavy qualification. Beyond a certain point it has no meaning, for bacteria are not individuals as you and I are individuals, or even as the members of a shoal of fish are individuals, because they share their genes so freely. In some senses you might describe all the world's bacteria as one single organism. Some scientists have suggested that this fact means we should abandon the entire taxonomic system by which bacteria are given names. The system cannot be applied to bacteria, all of which should be given a single name.

Bacteria have followed an evolutionary path that is radically different from the path leading to the large animals and plants we see around us. It has cost them their individuality, but if that was the cost, there was also a benefit, for it has gained them a kind of immortality. Individual cells die, of course, but since they reproduce simply by dividing into two daughter cells, each of which is identical in every way to the parent, just what is it that dies? Just as you cannot talk of a bacterium as an individual, you cannot talk of the death of a bacterium, for the first bacterium ever to appear on Earth is still here, and will remain until all life here ends. It was the first, and you may be sure it will be the last. It is mainly the bacteria, of course, on which we rely for the cycling of materials.

SIMPLE CELLS AND COMPLEX CELLS

Bacteria form one community, perhaps of global proportions, and plants and animals form smaller communities of cells, but their cells are different. A typical cell from a human body is about one thousand times larger than a bacterial cell, and it is a great deal more complicated.

Its nucleus, containing almost all of the cell's genes, is enclosed in a membrane and the cell contains other components, organelles, that have specific functions within the cell. Some organelles have genes of their own. A bacterial cell has no membrane enclosing a nucleus and no organelles. Cells without an enclosed nucleus, the simplest cells, are called prokaryotes; those with a membrane-bound nucleus, like all the cells in the body of a plant or animal, are eukaryotes.

Evolutionarily, the prokaryotes came first, as you would expect, but how did the first eukaryotes appear? A close study of the cells of the leaf of a green plant provides the most obvious clue. The cells, and the plant, are green because they contain chlorophyll, which is green, but the chlorophyll is not spread throughout the cell like a dye. It is contained in organelles, little packets, called chloroplasts.

Out in the open ocean, close enough to the surface to be exposed to sunlight, there are prokaryotes that contain chlorophyll. There are several types of chlorophyll, differing from one another chemically, and the chlorophyll in some of these prokaryotes is of the same type as that found in plants. These organisms are called prochlorophytes. They are extremely small. Some are less then one-thousandth of a millimetre across. They are also very abundant. In some places there may be as many as 100,00 of them in one millilitre of water (nearly 60 million in a pint).

At some stage organisms closely resembling present-day prochlorophytes entered other cells, or were ingested by them, and remained, being shared among the daughters when their hosts divided. In the course of time they lost their ability to live outside the host cells and these cells, with their chloroplasts, became the ancestors of the cells of green plants. Other cell organelles, some of them still containing fragments of their own genetic material, are believed to have originated in the same way. Flagella, the thread-like tails by which many cells propel themselves through the water, bear a strong resemblance to the spirochetes, thread-like bacteria, and may be descended from prokaryotes much like them.

A GLOBAL COMMUNITY

It took a long time for this collaboration to begin. The oldest fossils of what are undeniably eukaryotic cells are about 1,400 million years old, so they lived some 2,500 million years after life first appeared. They were photosynthesisers. The earliest non-photosynthesisers lived around 800 million years ago.

The joining together of eukaryotic cells to form larger organisms followed within about 100 million years. Some were, and still are, no more than loose confederations. The Portuguese man-o'-war, for example, looks like a jellyfish but is actually a colony of cells, each specialising in a particular function but still able to survive by itself. A sponge, too, is a simple colony. It can be smashed so its constituent cells separate and what was a sponge turns into cloudy water. Leave it alone and after a time the cells come together and the sponge forms itself again.

If I were asked to identify a single principle that seems to guide the development of life on Earth I would have to call it collaboration, the establishment of mutually supportive communities. You can find it at many levels. Simple, prokaryotic, apparently free-living cells are linked into some kind of super-organism. Other prokaryotes combined to form eukaryotic cells. Eukaryotic cells combined to produce larger, multicellular organisms, and multicelled animals tend to live in societies.

This view does not conflict with Darwinian evolution by

natural selection so much as add a further dimension to it. Evolutionary theory describes the relationships among and between species and their ancestors and the mechanisms by which species form. Gaian theory deals with the underlying organisation that produces individuals we can classify as species and the influence that organisation has on the planet as a whole. It deals, if you will, with the deep structure of evolutionary theory.

The old idea, of a world populated by essentially isolated individuals and dominated by conflict, is giving way to a new idea, of the world as a community. As it does so the concept of a living planet where organisms as a whole manage their total environment appears less preposterous than at first it may have seemed. Gaia becomes credible.

9
THE EARTH IS
NOT A GOD

When I am too hot I sweat. I may fan myself, look for a shadier spot in which to sit, or get myself a cold drink. I am aware of being too hot. Similarly, when I am cold I may turn on the heater or put on a sweater, and if I am very cold I may start to shiver. I know I am too cold. If the Earth is a single living being that regulates its own temperature it is tempting to assume that it, too, has a capacity to feel hot or cold. This may lead us to compare it with ourselves or with other animals, and then to jump to a wrong conclusion. Such an Earth must be sentient, if we apply the literal meaning of the word. There can be no response to a stimulus unless that stimulus is detected, and detection requires detectors, another word for senses. Sentience, the possession of senses, suggests some level of awareness, and awareness suggests consciousness. Gaia begins to resemble an intelligent being.

It is hardly surprising, therefore, that given a very brief and simplified outline of this new view of the way the planet works, together with a name to attach to it, that some people may come to regard Gaia as a god. Not only is this incorrect, it is potentially harmful. The apparently persuasive line of reasoning that leads to this interpretation is false. Gaia, or the Earth, is not intelligent, does not think, and most emphatically is not a god. To this extent the name Gaia is perhaps unfortunate.

SELF-ABSORPTION AND MORALITY

Most people, I think, would take the view that 'God' implies a being who is present, working in and through the lives of individual people. In part the concept is moral. God represents an ultimate and absolute good, in the moral sense, and is actively concerned for the moral welfare of humanity. Gaia, on the other hand, is wholly self-absorbed, a system whose only function is to continue functioning. The Gaian concept has no moral dimension unless you make the false assumption that Gaia is an intelligence, and in that case it is far from benign. This Gaia has no concern for human welfare, moral or even physical. From a Gaian point of view the prokaryotes I described in the last chapter are much more important than humans. Worship this 'god', therefore, and you worship something that is close to being the antithesis of what most people understand by the word 'God'. It leads to a pseudo-religion of despair, and that is harmful.

God, in most people's view, is omnipotent and omnipresent, not on Earth only but throughout the universe. Were there intelligent beings on some other planet, and there may be, God is as relevant to them as to us. In contrast, Gaia is no more than an aspect of the planet Earth, a way of describing the way things are. If other planets support life, no doubt it works there in a way similar to that which we find on Earth, but it is separate. There is no communication between Earth and other planets, no direct link beyond our belief that the laws of nature apply throughout the universe. On any planet, material objects released above the surface will fall to the surface because gravity applies everywhere. If planets support life, the Gaian view holds that they must do so in certain ways because the laws governing the relationships between organisms and their planets also apply everywhere. If you worship Gaia, what prevents you worshipping gravity?

Awareness of the concept may influence the way we behave in relation to the planet, and perhaps to one another, but its contribution is somewhat technical and in no sense moral. I shall try to outline some of this technical contribution towards the end of this chapter and in the final chapter. The contribution may be valuable, but at no point does it lead us to conclude that what we used to believe to be wrong can be seen to be right, or what was thought to be right in fact is wrong. It tells us we should respect the planet we inhabit, but we knew that already. Its contribution is to make that respect, what a Christian might call our stewardship, more effective.

MAGIC AND PSEUDORELIGION

Unhappily, these days pseudoreligions are thriving in Europe and North America. Many of them are based on fanciful interpretations of supposed pre-Christian beliefs which feature Earth mothers and Earth spirits, along with rituals that are supposed to persuade these beings to intervene in natural events, and largely because of the use of the name Gaia there is a serious risk of this concept being drawn into them. Some people believe that this so-called worship of the Earth may improve the relationship between people and the natural, non-human environment. Others may not go so far, but nevertheless regardless the new-old religions as well-meaning and harmless. I disagree. I think they are based on a false perception of reality that leads to a wilful ignorance of the natural world and that they are positively and seriously harmful to their practitioners and to the causes they pretend to support. They are more likely to cause injury than benefit to the natural environment and they certainly harm those who accept them as truth and inevitably feel betrayed and abandoned when their beliefs fail them.

My objection centres on the fact that the beliefs are founded not on any seriously religious view but on a belief in magic. The magician believes the world is operated by unseen but intelligent forces. These forces can be persuaded or coerced into producing desired effects, by changing the weather, for example, or healing the sick. Communication with these forces involves rituals that sometimes appear to succeed because mere probability ensures that desired outcomes follow on some occasions. Such 'success' seems to prove the efficacy of the ritual, but failure implies no more than an inadequate or incorrectly performed ritual. So the ritual becomes increasingly elaborate and those adhering to it are drawn ever more deeply into a view of the world that is internally consistent but that diverges rapidly from reality and from which they may find it difficult to escape. Apart from the injuries they suffer when their magic fails to manipulate a really important detail of reality, such as a serious organic illness, their view of the world excludes serious thought, replacing it with a sentimental cosiness in which non-humans are reduced to the status of subhumans that can be talked to, perhaps, but not studied because they are manipulated by capricious forces whose behaviour is necessarily unpredictable. In seeking what is false, those who adhere to such beliefs blind themselves to what is true and this I regard as offensive.

The scientific ideas I am describing in this book have nothing whatever to do with such views as these. Gaia is not an intelligent being, not a god, not anything you can talk to, pray to, or hope to influence by persuasion or ritual. I often wonder why people bother to seek the supernatural when the natural world is so filled with beauty and, surely, with marvels enough to satisfy the most voracious spirit. Beside the real world the imagined world of the occult is so pale and sterile, so unutterably dull. This is not to say the concept lacks religious implications. You may well see and welcome it as further information about the way God chooses that the world should be.

FINAL CAUSES

I hope I may have rescued the Gaian concept from one set of misunderstandings. There have been others, however, somewhat akin to these. They have been voiced as scientific criticism and they must be answered. The theory has been accused by scientists of being teleological, and that is something no scientific theory is allowed to be.

Teleology is a doctrine that explains phenomena by reference to final causes directed to some purpose. If I cut a plank of wood to a certain, measured length, for example, the immediate or efficient cause of the plank being reduced from its original length to one that is shorter can be explained with reference to the saw and the movements of my arm. The final cause must refer to my intention to add one more rickety bookcase to the wobble of shelving that precariously accommodates my books. Most human actions can be explained fully only if such final causes are taken into account because when you or I perform an act usually we do so for a reason, that is, to achieve some objective. This line of reasoning is perfectly legitimate when applied to the actions of people, but on no account may you apply it to events or phenomena in which humans are not directly involved.

Scientists devote a great deal of their time and attention to the study of causes and effects, trying to discover why things happen as they do. Causes produce effects, and therefore the cause must precede the effect. When I build what I choose in my vanity to call a bookcase, the project begins inside my head with a vision of the bookcase I plan to build (or wish I knew how to build). That is the final cause, it precedes the effect (the actual construction and the finished article) and all is well. We all know what is happening in this case. With phenomena that do not involve humans, however, we cannot be aware of any such final cause, we can find no plan for the project. All we have are the events we observe, proceeding in steps from cause to effect. If we suppose a final cause, we are saying, in effect, that a desired outcome in the future is determining present events. We can believe that the future is conditioned by the past, but how can the present be conditioned by the future? Causality is being made to run backwards, with effects determining causes. So any such idea must be rejected and it must be rejected firmly, because we really can use final causes in respect of our own actions and so it is very easy for any of us to slip into treating the non-human world according to the same standard. It is an intellectual trap into which many people have fallen.

If there is such a plan, in the mind of God perhaps, we can know nothing of it and we cannot investigate it the way we can ask another human what they are doing and why they are doing it. You cannot interrogate God, and so the introduction of God may make for an interesting metaphysical argument but it does not help scientifically. Science can deal only with what can be observed.

The critics believe the Gaian proposal falls into this trap, that it implies one or more final causes that cannot exist unless we also suppose an intelligence in whose mind such causes reside. Gaia begins to sound suspiciously like a god.

The Gaian concept is of a planet in which physical events are regulated by living organisms in such a way as to maintain living conditions those organisms can tolerate. But how can this be? How can bacteria 'know' there is a surplus or deficiency of this or that in some other part of the world and set themselves to doing something about it? How can the seaweeds 'know' that unless they pump iodine into the air the people far inland will end up thick-necked and stupid? That is one line of scientific criticism. A second line suggests that, even if such things could be, we are proposing a quite unreasonable degree of altruism. Organisms, according to most evolutionary biologists, are concerned only with their own survival. Where altruism occurs, as in instances I mentioned earlier of collaborative hunting, the sharing of food, or warning others of danger, the altruists benefit in the long run. If I issue the warning today I run a risk, but tomorrow someone else will issue the warning that will save me. It is a case of you scratch my back and I'll scratch yours.

WHY COLLABORATE?

Let me deal with the second criticism first. Why should organisms collaborate? A clue to this may be found in game theory, and in particular in studies of non-zero sum games. I should explain that game theory is a branch of statistics — the study of probabilities — that uses imagined contests to test the outcome of situations. Most of the games with which we are familiar involve a contest in which one person or team wins and the other loses. If you award a score of +1 to the winner and −1 to the loser, add the final scores together and the sum is 0. That is a zero sum game.

Other games are more complicated. Imagine a game that lasts for an indeterminate time. When you start you have no idea when it will end and it is best to assume it will continue for the rest of your life. In its simplest form, imagine a series of transactions in which you trade with a partner. There are two labelled boxes, one for each player. One player approaches the boxes, opens his or her own and either puts something in it or does not, then opens the other and removes whatever it contains. The second player follows and does the same. Neither player is allowed to observe the other and each player must deal with his or her own box before opening the other. At the end of each round, if both players have full boxes they are awarded 2 points each. If one leaves an empty box and the other a full box, 4 points are awarded to the recipient of the full box and −1 to the recipient of the empty box. If both boxes are empty the players get 0 points each.

If you were playing the game, what would you do? If you put something in your box but your opponent leaves you nothing, you score −1 and your opponent 4. If you leave your own box empty, either the box you open will contain something, in which case you score 4 and your opponent −1, or it will be empty, in which case you both score 0 but at least you have not lost. Clearly, then, the sensible thing is to leave an empty box. This is called defecting, but the rules permit it.

TIT FOR TAT

In 1979 Robert Axelrod of the University of Michigan at Ann Arbor invited game theorists to write computer programs that would play this game against a human partner or against other programs. The invitation led to an extended contest, involving a large number of people, from children to university professors, computer programs that were run hundreds of times against one another, and eventually to a book, *The Evolution of Cooperation*, by Axelrod. The implications for the evolution of behaviour have been studied in great detail.

The winning strategy, that survived more contests than any other, indeed that cannot lose, is so simple it was contained in the shortest computer program of them all, just a few lines long. It was devised by Anatol Rapoport of the University of Toronto, and is called tit for tat. In the first round you leave a full box. In each subsequent round you do whatever your partner did last time. If you open a full box, next time leave a full box. This is called being nice. If you open an empty box, next time leave an empty box. This is called being easily provoked.

In later rounds of this tournament, when contestants had been informed of earlier results and entries became more sophisticated, tit for tat continued to win. The lesson to be learned from it is that in any interactive situation the strategy that is most successful in the long run is to be cooperative and honest, respond to honesty in others, and if you are cheated respond at once in kind but then forgive immediately. When this kind of behaviour was tested against others it was easy to recognize, impossible to deceive, and so it encouraged cooperation from those that played with it. Evolutionarily, it means that collaboration is a necessary mathematical consequence of social interactions. It is not in the least remarkable to find organisms collaborating. They have no alternative because in any long-term competition for limited resources those that collaborate will survive and the selfish defectors eventually are bound to fail and disappear.

This explains the apparent paradox of collaboration. It also requires us to look again at our ideas of competition. We do not need computer programs to tell us that it is immoral to grab as much as we can for ourselves, to be greedy and selfish. We have always known that, and arguments to the contrary by some modern political theorists ring false. What the computer programs tell us is that such a strategy is not only morally indefensible; evolutionarily it is also self-defeating and leads ultimately and inevitably to the extinction of those who pursue it. Once again, it is not quite the meek who inherit the Earth, but at least it is the honest, and to our 'survival of the socially cohesive' we can add 'social cohesion is based on cooperation'.

CAUSALITY AND PROPENSITY

What, then, of the charge that the Gaian concept proposes causal relationships that run backwards?

At the World Philosophy Conference held in Brighton, England, in August 1988, Sir Karl Popper delivered a lecture in which he developed ideas he first published 30 years earlier that challenge some older ideas about causality.

When we think of a cause producing an effect we suggest a rather mechanistic universe in which, if you like, we are all being pushed into the future by whatever happened in the past. This happens in particular cases, of course, but Popper argued that such cases are comparatively rare. The more usual situation is that in which several outcomes are possible from a given starting point but only one of them can be realised.

If we are to discover which outcome is the most likely we must use a statistical method and when we do this, over many instances, we find that although several outcomes may be possible they are not equally probable. There is, Popper says, a propensity for a particular outcome to be realised, and there is a degree of propensity in every possibility. Each event produces new possibilities and propensities for future events. These are potentially real and it is they that drive the development of the world and the universe. Instead of being pushed along helplessly by what happened in the past, we are drawn — Popper uses the word 'enticed' — by the possibilities and propensities we see unfolding before us. This is true not only for you and I, making deliberate human choices, but for everything, and most especially for all living organisims. Popper sees the evolution of life in terms of the preference of organisms for certain of the possibilities available to them.

Without wishing to attribute to him opinions he may not hold, I must say that Sir Karl seems to me to have modified our ideas about causality in a most Gaian way. Gaia can be defended intellectually, but this contribution strengthens the defence.

DAISYWORLDS

I can turn now to the teleological objection. How can organisms predict the outcome of what they do and choose to do what is most beneficial to the community at large? Faced with this question, Jim Lovelock also resorted to his computer, but this time to play games of a different kind. He invented planets and called them daisyworlds because the only things that live on them are daisies.

The first and still the largest claim made for Gaia is that living organisms regulate the global climate, so Lovelock's experiments concentrated on climate regulation. They might equally have dealt with the cycling of chemical elements or any other kind of Gaian regulation, for the principles involved are similar. Lessons from daisyworld models apply to all aspects of the Gaian system.

A daisyworld is a planet, much like Earth only simpler, that orbits a main-sequence star much like the Sun. The planet has an atmosphere, but one lacking greenhouse gases which would complicate the calculations by trapping heat radiated from the planet's surface. The amount of incoming heat a planet absorbs is determined by how reflective its surface is, a quality called its albedo that can be measured. If its colour is very light it will have a high albedo. A snow-covered surface has an albedo of up to about 80 per cent, written as 0.8. On a daisyworld the bare ground has an albedo of 0.4, so it absorbs 60 per cent of the warmth it receives.

Only daisies grow on a simple daisyworld, although

other inhabitants were added to later models. There are two kinds of daisies, dark and pale. The dark ones have an albedo of 0.2 and are almost black, the pale ones are almost white and have an albedo of 0.7. Dark or light, the daisies cannot grow at a temperature lower than 5°C (41°F) and they die if the temperature exceeds 40°C (104°F). They grow best at around 20°C (68°F).

Imagine, first, that the star radiates only weakly, so daisyworld is a cold place. The pale daisies reflect most of the warmth falling on them so they stay cold, too cold to grow. The dark daisies absorb more heat, are warmed, and as their temperature exceeds the threshold they start to grow. The pale flowers disappear before seeds can be produced, but the dark flowers produce seeds. The next season starts with more dark daisies than there were the previous season, and fewer pale daisies. As the years pass the dark daisies cover more and more of the surface at the expense of the pale daisies. This reduces the albedo of the planet as a whole by making the surface darker. More heat is absorbed, warming the ground and the air above it. The climate grows warmer.

As the star ages it radiates more heat, just as our own Sun has done, and the situation begins to change. The dark daisies absorb so much of the warmth falling on them that their temperature exceeds the upper threshold and they die. The pale daisies reflect more warmth so their temperature remains tolerable. They produce more seed and proliferate at the expense of the dark daisies and after some years their expansion increases the albedo of the planet. It reflects more of the incoming heat, the ground is cooled and so is the air in contact with it, and the climate either grows cooler or at least is prevented from growing hotter.

The point of this simple model is to demonstrate that for living organisms to regulate the climate it is not necessary for them to plan ahead, to have a goal toward which they strive, far less for their behaviour to be directed by some external intelligence. Their inevitable response to changing conditions is sufficient to produce the climatic effect.

WHAT ABOUT GREY DAISIES?

This was all great fun and very interesting, but sceptics pointed out what seemed to them to be a flaw. If some daisies are dark and others light they presumed these colours are due to pigmentation in daisies that without the pigmentation would be grey. The coloured daisies would have to devote some of their energy to producing pigment, but the grey daisies, needing no pigment, would be able to devote more of their energy to growing and reproducing. The grey daisies would have an inherent advantage. Before very long they would spread to cover the entire planet by a strategy something like the defecting strategy in the tit for tat game. So Jim Lovelock added grey daisies and imposed a 1 per cent 'tax' on the dark and pale daisies to cover the energy cost of their pigment. Then he ran the experiment again.

Daisyworld has a climate, with poles and an equator, so there are always places where temperatures are markedly higher or lower than the global average. Where temperatures remained fairly constant and close to the optimum growing temperature the grey daisies did well, but the dark and pale daisies survived in high and low latitudes where grey daisies found conditions too hot or too cold. When the star radiated more or less strongly, however, the grey daisies could do nothing about it. They had to take the climate as they found it. One or other of the coloured daisies, on the other hand, was able to prosper, and regulation of the climate continued.

Fired with enthusiasm for such sport, and equipped with a computer that could handle all the mathematics, Jim Lovelock added daisies of more and more colours, until there were 20, of shades between nearly black and nearly white. While temperatures remained moderate all colours thrived, but when the going became tough the darker or paler colours covered a bigger area. Climate regulation continued.

Then animals were added to the models. There were rabbits that ate daisies of any colour and foxes that hunted rabbits. Their presence made no difference to the ability of the daisies to regulate the climate. Then catastrophes were added, in the form of plagues that killed one-third of all the daisies. Even then the regulation of climate continued and the populations recovered rapidly.

MODELLING THE REAL WORLD

The daisyworld models set out to convince sceptics that a Gaian type of environmental regulation requires no advance planning, that the theory is not teleological, but as the work developed it began to do much more than that. Lovelock was applying what ecologists call the competitive exclusion principle. This states that where two or more species require a particular but limited resource, one species will be better adapted than the others and in time will replace them, so that in a stable environment with limited resources there can be only one species dependent on each resource.

The principle allows scientists to calculate the effects of competition between two species and also to model relationships between predators and their prey. The usual example used is that of rabbits and foxes that are assumed to subsist wholly on rabbits (which real foxes do not, of course). If the rabbit population increases there is more food for foxes and so more foxes are born. The foxes eat more rabbits, reducing the rabbit population, but then there is less food for foxes and so their population also falls.

If something happens to disrupt the relationship, however, there are problems. Suppose disease suddenly kills most of the rabbits, but the survivors are immune and so the population recovers? The fall in the rabbit population leads to a fall in the fox population. The rabbit population recovers, but now there are few foxes so rabbits can proliferate. With much more food for foxes, the fox population expands. This causes a decline in the rabbit population, followed by a decline in the fox population, and establishes an endless cycle of boom and bust in both populations.

Such cycles do occur in the real world, but only under particularly stressful conditions. In the Arctic, populations of lemmings and their predators are locked into this kind of relationship. In less extreme environments, however, stability returns to disturbed communities, usually quite rapidly, but until now it has been impossible to calculate mathematically just how this happens. The fault lies in the mathematics, not in the real world.

The daisyworlds provided the missing ingredient. Ecologists studying these problems had assumed the physical and chemical environment to be beyond the influence of living organisms. If it should change, the species had to respond, but their response did nothing to change the non-living environment itself. In the daisyworlds, where the living and non-living components are intimately related, no particular group can expand beyond a certain level because a point is reached at which its own proliferation renders its environment hostile to it. It is the relationship between living and non-living that brings stability.

COMPLEXITY AND STABILITY

The models explained another puzzle. Despite the view popular among conservationists, mathematical models suggest strongly that simple communities, with few species, are more stable than complex communities. In other words, ecological complexity is a positive disadvantage and produces fragile systems. This is so provided the community is allowed no direct influence on the conditions under which it exists. Allow it such influence, as in the daisyworlds, and a different picture emerges. In a daisyworld, the more species, or daisy shades, there are, the greater the subtlety and precision with which the climate is regulated. Dark and pale daisies can deal with major temperature changes, but in-between shades deal with the smaller changes. Complexity is an advantage, after all.

The living Earth is an intricate, subtle, self-regulating

system, but one that is wholly automatic and logically inevitable. Once life is established, planetary management necessarily follows. Admittedly, the concept is poetic. What it describes is beautiful and should inspire in us awe and delight as, step by step, we are brought to an understanding of its subtleties. To those receptive to religious teachings it may bring a deeper appreciation of the way God chooses that our world should function. Behind such interpretations, however, Gaia is a scientific concept, born of scientific inquiry, developed, criticised and defended with the intellectual rigour science demands. You may derive implications from it, but you must not read into it what is not there and is not meant to be there. In particular you must not ascribe to it the attributes of an intelligent being. Gaia is not a person, far less a god.

10
HOW PLANETS DIE

Whenever you use the word life you imply absence of death. You could more or less get rid of the word living and substitute the phrase 'not dead'. It would be a bit clumsy, and to those of us brought up on horror movies it might suggest that we are all undead vampires or zombies, but apart from that it would make sense in a somewhat negative, possibly depressing way. In all the discussions about Gaia, the living planet, Earth is contrasted, quite deliberately, with such dead planets as Mars and Venus. Illustrating this with what I called the two dog problem, I compared a dog that is dead with an otherwise similar dog that is not.

The word life has a further implication, however. It suggests a temporary condition. If you describe something as alive you imply that there was a time before it was alive and there will be a later time when it has ceased to be so. Anything that lives must die.

In the case of Gaia I have referred often to the first appearance of life, to the time before the planet came to life. In terms of universal history, if you accept that the universe came into existence about 15 billion of our solar years ago — a very approximate age that could be wrong by several billion years, but let it stand for the moment — then the 4 billion years during which Earth has supported life began when the universe was already about 11 billion years old. So there was quite a long time before life appeared, and it is perfectly natural and proper to ask whether there will be a time after Earth has ceased to support life. Clearly, the answer has to be affirmative and, that being so, we are entitled to ask how and when Gaia is likely to die.

CONSUMED BY THE RED GIANT

We are entitled to ask, but we are not entitled to an answer, for no one can know the future. All the same, we are not quite helpless. We cannot tell when a particular person will die, but we do know the life expectancy of people according to their sex and nationality. In the same way we know the life expectancy of a planet.

One day our Sun will have consumed so much of its fuel that it will begin to crush other elements. When this happens its life as a main sequence star will end and it will begin to expand, quite rapidly, into a red giant. Many details of the physics of this process are not well understood but the fact of it is clear. When it happens the inner planets, including Earth, will be engulfed.

Shortly before that event conditions on Earth will become intolerably hot. Complex organic molecules will start to disintegrate because the heat energy they receive will impart sufficient energy to break the bonds that hold together their constituent atoms. Then carbon will begin to burn, consuming the oxygen in the air and substituting carbon dioxide. At that stage all life will have ceased. This ultimate death is inevitable and it is likely to occur some 5 billion years from now. According to this prediction, therefore, the Earth is about halfway through its allotted span. It is middle-aged.

The realisation does not take us much further. Do you know what 5 billion is? So far as I am concerned it is no more than a big number, useful mathematically but with no real meaning. I can imagine a century. Some people I knew as a child were born in the 1870s, so I have a link of sorts to that time. I can even stretch my imagination to believe in people they knew as children, who must have been born around the beginning of the last century. With difficulty my brain can cope with a couple of centuries, but not with billions of years. Since we are into big numbers, though, we can try it another way. Let us be generous and assume humans have existed as a species for 2 million years. That gives us a kind of species age for our own kind, and it comes to 1/2, 500, or 0.04 per cent, of 5 billion. It gives you an idea of just how big a number a billion is and how recently humans appeared on the scene. Perhaps for this reason Jim Lovelock says we may as well forget all about Gaia ever dying. The prospect is so unimaginably remote as to be meaningless.

THE DEATH OF PLANTS

Five billion years is a maximum lifespan, however, and in the real universe things are not quite so simple. Other changes are taking place and we do not know how the planet will or can respond to them.

Our story began with the regulation of climate by living organisms. This was achieved through the removal of carbon dioxide from the atmosphere and the secure long-term storage of the carbon to produce the opposite of a greenhouse effect. For the entire history of our planet this has been effective and climates have remained tolerable, but we should not assume it can continue being effective for all eternity. What happens when carbon dioxide stocks run low?

According to some estimates, when life began on Earth carbon dioxide probably accounted for about 30 per cent of the volume of the atmosphere, or 300,000 parts of carbon dioxide to every million parts of the total atmosphere. Other scientists maintain the figure was much higher. Today the air contains about 300 parts per million of carbon dioxide, or 0.03 per cent. The Sun continues to grow hotter, but there is not much more carbon dioxide to remove. Almost all of it has already gone.

In fact it is worse than it looks because some of the organisms involved in removing carbon dioxide are green plants and they depend on it for their very existence. Remove much more and the plants will be unable to survive. Already it is fairly standard practice for commercial growers to enrich the air in their greenhouses with carbon dioxide to increase plant growth, suggesting that at least some plants in the open air could benefit from having more of the gas than is available to them now. Were the concentration reduced to about half its present level, around 150 parts per million, most plants would die.

This would impair the ability of organisms to regulate the temperature because at present, not counting human intervention, which I shall come to presently, the carbon cycle involving plants is in balance and that balance would be severely perturbed. Small animals and fungi that feed on dead plant material and bacteria would not be affected. They do not need carbon dioxide. Proliferating because the death of plants increased their food supply, they would decompose the material presented to them and release carbon dioxide, increasing the atmospheric concentration and allowing plants partly to recover. As the plants grew they would remove some of the carbon dioxide again, die, be decomposed, and so a cycle of fluctuations would begin that would cause associated fluctuations in the climate. Conditions would become warmer, then cooler. Volcanoes would continue to release carbon dioxide and with the rate of biological removal reduced it would add to the accumulation.

Fluctuations of this kind in a system usually mean its mechanisms for self-regulation are beginning to fail. If it is a living system you would say the condition of the patient is unstable, and as the fluctuations continued you would have to admit that it was close to death. In the case of the Earth, as the Sun's output continued to intensify, the climatic trend would be toward higher temperatures. At more than about 40°C (104°F) respiration ceases in many plants and they die, decomposing to release more carbon dioxide, leading to an accelerated warming, so that once the average temperature exceeds this value the planet warms much more quickly. The animals that feed on living plants will die before this stage is reached, of course. They will have starved.

This process will also affect the principal carbon-removers, in the oceans. As the amount of carbon dioxide decreases, less carbonate will be carried by rivers to the sea. There will be less for them, and so their numbers will decline, then increase again when carbon dioxide concentrations increase. They will join and add to the fluctuations.

The bacteria may survive, even at temperatures high enough to kill plants, for they are robust and adaptable. It may be, therefore, that the death of plants and animals would not mean the end of all life on Earth, or of Gaian planetary management. Life would continue under stable conditions but at a much higher temperature.

When will this happen? In theory it may be in about 100 million years from now. That, too, is an unimaginably long time in the future so far as you and I are concerned. It is much too remote to affect anyone directly related to us in any real sense. Yet in another way it is not so long. Look 100 million years into the past and you find the world populated by dinosaurs, flying reptiles, birds, fishes, the first mammals, and most of the invertebrate animals we know today. If you draw a line 2 feet long to represent the 5 billion years life has existed on Earth so far, a mark half an inch from the end will indicate that time 100 million years ago. Look at it this way and perhaps the Earth is not middle-aged after all. Perhaps it is very old indeed and close to the end of its life.

I said it may happen 'in theory' 100 million years from now. This indicates sensible caution, not that you will be around then to complain that the figure is wrong, nor I to hear your complaint. Caution is needed because for all we know some entirely novel system of regulation may come into operation to postpone Gaia's demise. Or something else may happen to aggravate the condition, so the end comes sooner.

THE TIME GAIA NEARLY COMMITTED SUICIDE

This sounds like an ominous threat, so before I go any further I had better provide some reassurance. Gaia is a great deal tougher than some people imagine. The planet will die one day, that is certain, but in the past it has survived assaults so appalling as to suggest it can withstand almost anything.

Environmentalists are sometimes distressed by the phrase 'natural pollution'. It suggests to them that people who use it, as I do, believe that pollution of the environment by humans is natural and therefore acceptable. I mean nothing of the kind. If you accept that a pollutant is a substance introduced to the environment, or present in an unusually large concentration, that can have an adverse effect on living things, then it is clear that humans are not the only polluters. Volcanoes are major polluters, for example. This does not excuse careless factory owners. Let me tell you a pollution horror story.

I have made much of the way carbon dioxide was removed from the air. So far as life on Earth was concerned, this was obviously beneficial, but a price had to be paid and it was a very high price indeed. The process began with the marine organisms and carbon-rich sediments, but it was not long before photosynthesis began, spread rapidly, and removed a large amount of carbon dioxide in quite a short period. A byproduct of photosynthesis is free oxygen, released into the air or water. It seems strange to us, because without free oxygen we die in a very few minutes, but oxygen was the pollutant, and to some extent it still is.

In the world prior to the emergence of photosynthesis, free gaseous oxygen was extremely rare and none of the organisms living at the time had the slightest use for it. Indeed, so far as they were concerned it was a very dangerous poison. Oxygen reacts readily with most substances and so it can disrupt chemical reactions that are not meant to involve it. Oxygen accumulated in the atmosphere until, perhaps quickly, the entire chemistry of the environment altered. Over the entire planet the air became poisonous.

The devastation must have been on a truly vast scale, yet life did not vanish. Many organisms survived in places where oxygen could not penetrate, such as dense muds permanently covered with water. Other organisms adapted to tolerate the oxygen by making use of it as a source of energy. They allowed it to react chemically, but under circumstances they controlled. In time, as large animals evolved, some of the organisms that to this day cannot tolerate oxygen came to live inside the animal bodies. They make it possible for termites to digest wood, cattle and sheep to digest grass, and they flourish in your guts and mine helping us digest our food and producing some of the vitamins we must have.

What happened all that time ago was catastrophic. It was by far the most serious 'pollution incident' the world has ever known. Yet, far from destroying life, it was followed by a great proliferation of life. Many species must have been sacrificed, but the planet as a whole, Gaia, prospered.

The effects are with us still, for oxygen has lost none of its reactivity and a substantial part of the body chemistry in animals is devoted to rendering it harmless, with only partial success. Oxygen-based reactions release even more reactive molecules (radicals) that can interfere with the functioning of cells, leading to cancer in precisely the same way that ionising radiation does. This may place an upper limit on the lifespan of animals based on the rate at which they use oxygen to produce energy. Small mammals, for example, use oxygen more rapidly than large animals, and do not live so long. A hamster may live for less than two years, a mouse for three and a horse for 60. Extend these spans much further and cancer becomes almost unavoidable because of the amount of oxygen to which the animal has been exposed. This probably means that talk of extending the human lifespan much beyond its present value is mere fantasy.

ASSAULTS OCCASIONING GRIEVOUS BODILY HARM

The Earth may be self-regulating but it is not alone, not immune from outside interference. In the summer of 1988, at the Siberian Institute of Technology in Krasnoyarsk, a symposium was held to mark the anniversary of a strange event. Eighty years before, at Tunguska in a sparsely populated region of Siberia, a large area of forest was, quite literally, flattened, with the trees lying in such a way as to suggest they had been uprooted by a single violent explosion. There was no crater, the trees were not burned, so far no remains have been found of whatever may have caused the explosion. To this day no one is entirely certain what happened, but the most likely explanation is that part of a comet, made principally of ice, entered the atmosphere and exploded before it reached the ground. The solar system is less tranquil than it may seem and living in it is not entirely safe.

In the early 1980s Jim Lovelock and I collaborated in writing a book called *The Great Extinction.* It dealt with a somewhat similar but much bigger catastrophe. At the time we wrote the book its central theme was more controversial than it is now. Today most scientists accept that 65 million years ago a planetismal — a piece of rock of uncertain origin — about 10 or 11 kilometres (6 or 7 miles) across and with a weight variously estimated at between 100 billion and 1,000 billion tons, or by another scientist at 2,500 billion tons, collided with the Earth with an impact speed of about 20 kilometres per second, or almost 45,000 miles per hour. The violence of that impact was roughly equivalent to detonating at least 1,000 times the world's entire nuclear stockpile, all at once and all in one place.

What happens when something that big hits the Earth that hard? We know that the impact coincided with the extinction of about 70 per cent of all species living at the time it happened. Yet the planet recovered, and it recovered rapidly. Once the immediate effects were past, species proliferated, new species evolved and mammals thrived. Until then they had been small, rather undistinguished animals. The catastrophe ushered in what some people have called the age of mammals.

CAN YOU KILL A PLANET?

The effects of that catastrophe were felt in every part of

the world, and as we worked on our book we had to
speculate about what those effects may have been. No one
really knows, of course, because no one has ever witnessed
such an event. Obviously nothing could have survived
anywhere close to the site of the impact, but what
happened further afield?

We tried out various theories. Did dust from the impact
blot out sunlight sufficiently to reduce photosynthesis, kill
plants, and so starve animals? Were there vast fires that
destroyed vegetation over huge areas and contributed to
the darkness? (There is now some evidence of such fires.)
Did the amount of energy released in the atmosphere
cause so much nitrogen to be oxidised that rain water
contained enough nitric acid to kill plants? Did poisons
from the object itself kill plants and animals? Did the
sudden destruction release vast quantities of organic
matter into the oceans, effectively poisoning them?

We cannot know, but as we speculated we found
ourselves wondering what it would take for human
intervention to kill so robust a planet. One by one we went
through the possibilities and one by one we rejected them.
The greatest possible self-inflicted disaster we could
imagine then was all-out thermonuclear war, but even that
would not destroy life, or even render humans extinct,
although almost certainly it would destroy all our political
and social institutions. Life for the survivors would be very
unpleasant indeed, but there would be survivors and
within less than a century there would be little biological
evidence of what had happened. The plants and animals
would suffer no serious long-term harm. The Pacific atolls
where hydrogen bombs were tested for a number of years
were stripped not only of all plants and animals but of
their soil as well, blasted away, leaving the bare coral
exposed. After atmospheric testing ended it was not long
before they were recolonised.

We became deeply sceptical of predictions of imminent
doom, mainly because most of them are based on a kind of
frontal assault on the planet. There really is no way
humans could blast, burn, irradiate or even poison a large

enough proportion of living things to make recovery impossible once the abuses ceased. Again, this statement is often misunderstood. It does not mean the Gaia idea implies absolute freedom for people to do as they like with impunity, for there are other values to be considered. Jim Lovelock and I both love the countryside and its wildlife and are deeply offended when large tracts are converted into tedious agricultural or afforested monocultures. We object strongly to the pollution of rivers and the persecution of species, even those designated 'pests'. Such insults will not destroy the planet, but this does not make them acceptable or harmless. An assault does not have to be fatal before we condemn it.

A FEVERED EARTH?

Yet there are ways in which our behaviour may cause severe damage, subtly, by disturbing the Earth's regulatory mechanisms and in particular by interfering with the climate. It is time to say a little more about the greenhouse effect.

Not many years ago most climatologists were predicting an ice age and some were saying a little ice age was likely in the very near future. Now they are warning of a warming, so which set of predictions should we believe? Curiously enough, both are correct. Until recently average global temperatures were falling and it looked as though they would continue to do so. Then the trend was reversed, so now we appear to be warming. The greenhouse effect appears to be overriding an underlying trend toward cooler conditions.

Some caution is necessary because trends in global temperatures are very difficult to detect. Climates change over long periods, for example between ice ages and interglacials. Within those large cycles there are changes that last for shorter periods. The little ice age that gripped the northern hemisphere for several centuries and ended about 100 years ago is a fluctuation of this kind. Within these cycles there are still shorter ones, of runs of warm and cool years. The possible range of such quite ordinary variations is considerable. This means that any change has to be maintained over a sufficient number of years for it to be clear that it is out of the ordinary. At present there is no doubt that average temperatures are rising, but it will be some years yet before scientists will be able to say confidently that the warming is due to the greenhouse effect.

Over the last century the concentration of carbon dioxide in the atmosphere has increased by 25 per cent and at present it is rising by about 1.5 per cent each year. About 20 billion tons of the gas are released annually by the burning of wood, peat, coal, oil and natural gas, some 25 per cent of it in the USA, 22 per cent in the USSR and 15 per cent in Western Europe. More carbon dioxide is released when tropical forests are cleared, partly through the decomposition or burning of the vegetation but mainly because the air trapped among soil particles contains much more carbon dioxide than atmospheric air, and when forests are cleared this soil air is likely to be released.

Carbon dioxide traps long-wave radiation from the ground surface, but it is not the only gas to do so. Methane does so, and its concentration is also increasing, produced mainly by cattle and wet rice cultivation. Nitrogen oxides, produced mainly by car exhausts, trap heat, and so do the chlorofluorocarbons used as propellants in some aerosol cans, as refrigerants in refrigerators, freezers and air conditioners, and in some foam plastics.

This is subtle pollution, for the substances involved are not what most people think of as pollutants. Carbon dioxide and methane poison nothing. By themselves they are innocuous. Chlorofluorocarbons are blamed for depleting the stratospheric ozone layer, but the chemicals themselves are so non-toxic you could drink large amounts of them and come to no harm. Even nitrogen oxides contribute useful nutrients to the soil.

Most large-scale studies into the effect of these releases predict a rise in the average global temperature in the fairly near future and some scientists believe that rise, and some of its consequences, are with us already. In the world as a whole, the 1980s have been unusually warm, rainfall patterns have been changing and, at a scientific meeting held in 1987, Wayne Evans of the Atmospheric Environment Service of Environment Canada said he had measured a 0.1 per cent increase since 1975 in the amount of radiation being retained by the Earth. The drought in the Sahel region of Africa in the early 1980s, and in 1988 the·drought in North America and floods in the Sudan and Bangladesh have been said to be consistent with the predicted greenhouse effect.

If the gases implicated in greenhouse warming continue to accumulate in the atmosphere, clearly we may expect major changes in climates, although at present no one can say with any certainty what those changes will entail. Some areas may become drier, some wetter, most warmer but not all warming at the same rate. Western Europe is warming relatively slowly, for example, and while much of the world may have been experiencing hot, dry summers, when the temperature rises in the surface waters of the Atlantic, Western Europe has cool, wet summers. Sea levels are rising because, being warmer, the seas have expanded, and the melting of the Antarctic ice sheets will raise them much further. Some scientists believe they have measured the start of that melting.

CAN THE BALANCE BE RESTORED?

The problem must be taken seriously, but I am concerned here not so much with ways in which humans may cope with it as with the way the planet itself may cope with it, and curious things are happening. Satellite photographs and research ships reveal that the number of coccolithophorids has increased dramatically. Vast clouds of them have been seen in the central North Atlantic.

Minute, plant-like organisms classified as algae, coccolithophorids form part of the phytoplankton, the small plants that drift near the surface of the sea. They are covered in plates, called coccoliths, made from calcium carbonate and they have always been one of the principal groups involved in capturing and burying carbon.

Other algal blooms have occurred in the northern North Sea. In 1988 they were widely reported because as they died and decomposed the water around them was depleted of dissolved oxygen and many fish died. The algae were regarded as a pollution problem in themselves and as the result of a pollution problem, in that the discharge of plant nutrients, principally nitrogen, from European rivers was believed to have caused their proliferation. This may be, but the blooms had been recorded for several years previously and they may be associated with warmer water.

At the same time more dimethyl sulphide (DMS) is being emitted, especially in the tropics and subtropics, but also by the North Sea algae. Some planktonic species release more DMS than others and the coccolithophorids release much more than most. The DMS is released into the water. Some escapes into the air directly, some is chemically broken down first, partly by bacteria, but in the air it is oxidised to produce particles of sulphate on to which water vapour can condense. As the atmosphere warms, more water evaporates from the sea. Water vapour itself is a greenhouse gas, but once the vapour condenses to form clouds it has a cooling effect. The clouds shade the surface and the cloud tops, shining brilliantly in the sunlight, reflect incoming radiation, increasing the overall albedo of the planet.

This looks very much like a biological response to rising temperature, a Gaian mechanism for offsetting the greenhouse warming. The organisms involved are being wholly selfish, of course. They have nothing you could call an intention to benefit the world, and in responding to change in an entirely automatic way they are the first beneficiaries. The clouds shade them, especially from ultraviolet radiation which may be slightly injurious to them, and if the clouds are associated with thunderstorms the rainfall brings them some nitrogen, which is all to their good. Nitrogen oxides emitted by factories may also aid the process by drifting over the sea and being washed down in rain.

This helps to explain the cool, wet summers experienced in northern Europe for several years in succession. It also explains some, probably most, of the acid rain problems of Europe and North America. The clouds forming over the oceans are composed of water droplets condensed on to sulphate particles, so the water is dilute sulphuric acid.

COPING WITH HARD TIMES

A rise in temperatures sufficient to lead to a melting of the polar ice will cause a rise in sea levels and the flooding of low-lying coastal areas, reducing the total area of dry land. The oceans being larger, it is possible that more DMS may be released, producing a cooling effect. Conversely, during an ice age sea levels fall, more land is exposed, and with a smaller sea area less DMS may be released, reducing cloudiness and favouring a general warming.

A trend toward cooler conditions seems an appropriate response to increasing output from the Sun and the evidence suggests that during the last few tens of millions of years an ice age is the normal condition on Earth. Warmer periods, with less ice or none, occur when there is a failure in the regulatory system. Until now the situation has corrected itself.

During an ice age the air contains less carbon dioxide. Since carbon dioxide is removed by living organisms, it follows that there must be more biological activity during an ice age than at other times. There is only one region in which this activity can be located — the tropics, where large areas of silt-laden and fertile land are exposed as the sea level falls. It is reasonable to suppose that, if it is through biological activity that tolerable conditions are maintained, then the more plants and animals there are, and the greater their diversity, the better chance there will be of surviving hard times.

A disturbing picture begins to emerge. The output of energy from the Sun increases steadily, tending to warm the Earth. Carbon is removed from the air and buried to counteract the warming. When the carbon dioxide level falls very low, from time to time there is too little to prevent the slight additional cooling that triggers an ice age, but in a Gaian sense a cool Earth is much healthier than a warm one. As recently as the 1960s and early 70s average temperatures were falling gradually in the northern hemisphere, and probably in the southern as well. That is why climatologists were predicting a return to much colder conditions. By releasing carbon dioxide and other greenhouse gases, however, we are now overriding the system. We are encouraging a warming at a time when the Earth should be cooling and so exacerbating a natural problem. It is no wonder that scientists now take the greenhouse effect very seriously indeed. For those of us living in cool, damp Britain the prospect of a Mediterranean climate may sound inviting. We should not deceive ourselves. We would have to find homes for the large numbers of people migrating from low-lying areas, especially in eastern England, as their land was submerged as a result of rising sea levels, and we could not isolate ourselves from the still greater disruption and distress in other parts of the world.

It may be that the planet is preparing itself in other ways for the increasing output from the Sun. Within the last 40 million years or so a new group of plants, the grasses, has appeared and spread rapidly. Some of the more recently evolved grasses, mainly the cane-like ones such as sugar cane and corn (maize), photosynthesise in a slightly different way from other plants, using carbon dioxide much more efficiently. This enables them to grow well where carbon dioxide concentrations are low, as they are in clearings in tropical and subtropical forests, for example, where trees absorb much of the available carbon dioxide. As the amount of carbon dioxide continues to fall, such plants will prosper. In the end, though, they can do no more than postpone the crisis, for despite their efficiency they must have some carbon dioxide and the time will come when a temperature tolerable to plants can be maintained only with an atmosphere containing no carbon dioxide at all. Eventually the plants must lose.

Our devotion to burning fuels containing carbon and our clearance of tropical forests are potentially very dangerous indeed. The planet needs to be cooled so its biological activity may increase in order to offset the slow but steady rise in solar output. As I have explained, our release of carbon dioxide and other greenhouse gases is now overriding and reversing that trend; not merely interrupting the cooling process but actually causing a warming.

If this interpretation of events is correct we may have more to worry about than floods, droughts and failed crops. We may be destabilising the global climate at a time when it is beginning the long struggle to retain stability in the face of deteriorating circumstances. Perhaps the doomsayers are wrong and the threat is exaggerated, but should we take such a risk when the stakes are so high?

11
A PLACE FOR PEOPLE

There are a few very fundamental questions that have haunted people throughout the whole of recorded history and probably since our species first appeared. They all centre around ourselves and the purpose of our lives. Who are we? Why are we here?

It is easy to romanticise this search for identity and purpose, to assume that, because it has troubled thinkers, therefore it has been of concern to everyone. We have a delightfully sentimental picture of our early ancestors, wrapped in animal skins, the men usually with neatly trimmed beards and hairstyles that would do them credit in London or New York, leaning on their spears and gazing reflectively at the star-clad night sky as they wondered about the purpose of it all. Probably they were depressed. If you ask me, most people have spent most of their time trying to make a living and if they did any wondering at all it was about how they were going to pay for the groceries. The thinkers were a privileged few who left their wives to do the worrying part of the wondering. Xanthippe, the wife of Socrates, achieved immortality by refusing to play the game.

The questions, to the extent that we are supposed to take them seriously, are concerned with the proper or underlying relationship between humans, the world and the universe. I have been describing a new perception of the way the world works and, to some extent, of its relationship to the universe. Sooner or later it was inevitable that the old questions would reappear. What part do humans play in all this? If the Earth is a living organism, if the Gaian idea is even approximately true, where do you and I fit into the great scheme of things?

DOES GAIA HAVE A BRAIN?

Ask someone this question, and after a brief pause for thought the answer is likely to be that we humans are the brain of Gaia, the organ that does the thinking. It is an obvious answer from a member of the species that calls itself *sapiens*, but clearly it is wide of the mark.

We believe that humans are unique. It is true, of course, but the fact gets you nowhere. Every species is unique because that is how the word 'species' is defined. We may seem special because we have no close relatives, but this is irrelevant, and in any case it is untrue. Our close relatives are the chimpanzees and gorillas. They are very different from us but that rather uninteresting observation merely takes us back to the definition of a species. We can tell the difference easily enough, but would a visitor from some remote galaxy find it so easy, especially if there were more or less equal numbers of all three species? There are two species of seals living around the shores of Britain, the common or harbour seal and the grey seal. You need to know quite a lot about seals to tell which is which, but the seals have no problem. They can tell the difference and seals are every bit as entitled as you or I to regard their own kind as unique or special.

Some people suggest humans are special because, unlike other species, we are intensely social but, as I pointed out earlier, almost all animals are social. Studies of animal behaviour, not to mention Gaian theory, affirm that sociability is the rule rather than the exception. Consider the complex networks of relationships that form within a herd of horses, with often lifelong friendships and enmities, elaborate rituals when meeting strangers, and, most convincing of all, the depression that almost always results when a horse is forced to live by itself rather than as a member of a herd. Any thoughts I may have about the intricacies of human societies are modified when I watch the committees of starlings feeding on the lawn and spending most of their time debating which morsel belongs to whom.

Nor can we claim that our social arrangements are uniquely based on a sophisticated means of communication. All societies must be so based or how could they function as societies? Consider the way a worker bee communicates to her colleagues the distance and location of a food source. Watch the communication, by scent, gesture, body posture and vocalisation, when two dogs meet in the park.

Are humans special because we are aware of ourselves as individuals, because of our self-consciousness? Most people believe we are, but I have grave doubts. No organism can survive unless it is able to distinguish between self and not-self, and animals go much further. They can identify other individuals and have attitudes towards those individuals. Some are known to be friendly, others are enemies to be avoided or intruding strangers to be investigated or repelled; as for other species some are dangerous, some are edible, others are neither and so of no interest. There must be some awareness of self to make this recognition possible. Whenever my human vanity leads me to suppose I am special or superior to all other animals, a few minutes watching the two cats who live in our home (or do we live in theirs?) correct me. There is not much doubt about how special they think they are, and we cannot all be right.

WHAT ARE BRAINS FOR?

If a particular species is to be the brains of Gaia it must have a better claim than I can make out for humans. Our brainpower is part of a continuum and all animals have brains of some kind. So far as we know there are no philosophers among other species, but this does not help much. Supposing it to be true, all it tells us is that a particular kind of activity is restricted to humans. Other activities are restricted to other species and are we entitled to regard such activities as less useful?

I would not go too far in debunking humans, although we certainly deserve it, for I will come later to the use I think I may have found for them. Meanwhile, let us stay a while longer with the subject of brains. The essential purpose of a brain is to coordinate the activities of its possessor. It receives sense impressions from the outside world, interprets them according to its inherited or acquired knowledge of the world, determines appropriate responses, directs the muscles that make those responses, and the rest of the time it governs the internal operations of the body. Without a brain you are dead because your body cannot function — the system fails. Individuals have brains from the moment they come into existence as independent beings.

This being so, and brains being so vital, how can it be that after all this time Gaia suddenly finds it necessary to recruit humans to that role? If an organism cannot function without a brain, how has Gaia managed until now? After all, we arrived on the scene very recently. Either brains are much less important than we thought, in which case Gaia has no need of one, or brains are as important as we thought, in which case Gaia must have had the equivalent of one from the start. Both arguments write humans out of the script.

What, though, if Gaia is suddenly awakening to a full consciousness of self? This, too, has been suggested. It is a happy suggestion because it seems to give us a part that is much more dignified than mere supervision of the digestive system. We are to be not the whole brain of Gaia but only the interesting part, the higher centres of that brain. We can concern ourselves exclusively with contemplation of the finer things in life.

Alas, beautiful though it is, the idea is badly flawed. It assumes that humans are better qualified for such a role than any other species; indeed that it was not until humans appeared that Gaia recognised the possibilities of such thought. In the first place, what right do we have to assume we are up to the job? In the second place, if Gaia has just realised these possibilities, with what organ did 'she' do this realising? You cannot recognise the value of having a brain unless you have a brain with which to do the recognising.

The more serious flaw lies in the attribution of personal qualities to a planet, the fallacy I spent Chapter 9 demolishing. Gaia is a system, complicated, beautiful, but nothing more than a system. It is not a person. The concept 'awakening to a full consciousness of self' is meaningless. There is neither a self nor anything to awaken to a consciousness of it.

DOES GAIA HAVE A CONSCIENCE?

Maybe, though, humans are the conscience, or moral awareness, of the planet? Since the dawn of our history we have had a religious and moral sense and you might argue that this has developed through earlier, more primitive stages to its present, advanced level. Surely, no animal is better qualified than we are for this role? This, too, has been suggested. It is the most delightful conceit yet, and takes our genius for self-deception to new and greater heights.

Consider Gaia as though it were a machine. Indeed, this is quite a rational way to think of it. It is a very complicated machine so, to make it easier, let us imagine a simpler machine, like a motor car. How can a motor car possess or have any need for a conscience or awareness of moral values? The driver of the car needs them, but it is ludicrous to apply the concept to the car itself. Applying it to the Earth implies, yet again, that we are thinking of the planet as though it were an intelligent being.

Our consciences should guide us in our dealings with one another and with the planet itself. To this extent they are of great importance. If we can supply them with sufficient accurate information, so they can provide us with informed guidance rather than haphazard hunches, they could allow us to live in greater harmony with our environment, both human and non-human. Doubtless we would have to reform ourselves and learn to behave better. We would have to stop doing those things that injure the planet and do other things that render us harmless. Such thoughts are very worthy but they apply to humans, to ourselves, not to any other species and not to the planet itself. It does not need to reform its behaviour. For us to cast ourselves in the role of the planet's conscience is rather like criminals appointing themselves judges, and the only judges at that.

The conclusion thus far is not very encouraging to our vanity. The self-regulating planet operates mainly through the prokaryotes, the simplest and smallest of cells. Green plants are also important and so are the minute coccolithophorids and other marine organisms that contribute to the burying of carbon. The planet has worked perfectly well at this level for thousands of millions of years and this is still the method it uses. There really is no need for large animals of any kind and certainly not for humans. If every last human were to vanish, the planet would carry on regardless. Indeed, it might well benefit from the cessation of those human activities that tend to perturb it. Gaia has no need of humans and perhaps it is better that we avoid asking about our part in the scheme of things. At best we have no part. We are no more than supernumeries, decorative spear carriers, filling the stage while the real actors get on with the play. At worst we are a kind of malignancy, multiplying too rapidly, destroying too much, a threat to the commonwealth of all life.

I cannot leave the matter here, of course, for there is another side to the debate. It is only when we arrogate to ourselves an inflated and quite unwarranted importance that we behave absurdly. We have positive qualities, too, and it would be unjust as well as misleading to ignore them. Not everything we do is bad, even from a Gaian point of view.

THE GREENING OF MARS

The concept of Gaia began when Jim Lovelock was working for the US space programme. It arose from space research and the link has never been broken. A few years ago he and I wrote another book, called *The Greening of*

Mars. The theme was Gaian. At one level we wanted to contrast environments on one planet that supports life and another that does not, to explore just what it is that constitutes a habitable environment. We could have written a rather dry, technical kind of book, but that would have conveyed nothing of the delight both of us feel when playing with ideas. So we performed a thought experiment and described it in semi-fictional terms, with a skeleton of a plot on to which we could hang scientific ideas and speculations.

We described the steps by which Mars might be transformed into a planet where humans could live. To do this we had to make a number of assumptions about the way Mars is. These could turn out to have been false, but if they were correct our scheme might actually work. It proved successful when it was tested in computer simulations, in Britain and the US, and it aroused considerable scientific interest when it first appeared.

We assumed that below the surface of Mars there is water, in the form of permafrost. We also assumed the atmosphere to consist mainly of carbon dioxide and the polar icecaps to be mainly solid carbon dioxide. Oxygen is plentiful on Mars, but not as a gas. It is combined, but loosely, in rocks and soil. Releasing it would present no great technical difficulties.

Our first step involved altering the climate. Mars is much too cold for comfort. So we fired rockets, obtained from the military as a byproduct of superpower disarmament, their warheads replaced by canisters of chlorofluorocarbons, very effective greenhouse gases. Having been banned on Earth, we imagined that companies paid to have the chlorofluorocarbons removed.

The rockets were designed only to hit Mars and release their payloads into the atmosphere, and the contents were doped with cultures of some very tough microorganisms, dark in colour and collected in Antarctica where they grow in places free from ice. The chlorofluorocarbons performed their greenhouse function, warming the air. This caused the solid carbon dioxide to evaporate, enhancing the greenhouse warming sufficiently to start melting some of the permafrost. Water vapour, also a greenhouse gas, then joined the other gases. Meanwhile the microorganisms, scattered on the surface, survived in a few places, began to spread, and, being dark, they reduced the planet's albedo.

Before long humans began to arrive, converting the ships that transported them into accommodation, workshops and factories, as well as greenhouses in which they could grow food, from seeds brought from Earth grown in Martian soil modified to make it tolerable and then mixed with soils from Earth to provide the necessary soil organisms. The colonists generated nuclear power but also used solar power, mainly to reflect warmth to the surface and accelerate the melting of the permafrost. They obtained their oxygen from rocks which also supplied metal ores and construction materials. Relying mainly on local materials, within a short time they were self-sufficient and could devote their surplus time and energy to working in the open, encouraging the alteration of the planetary surface.

By the end of the story, which we told in a kind of flashback, as though it were history, humans wearing breathing apparatus could walk in the open on Mars with no further protective clothing and in the middle of the day, near the equator, it was warm enough to go around in shirtsleeves. There were no oceans, there is not enough water for that, but there were shallow lakes, marshes and swamps. Plants were growing in most places in low latitudes.

What we had done, mentally at least, was to give Mars a jolt. We had made it warmer, then seeded it with life so the change could become self-sustaining. Without the living organisms the planet would have become warmer, but in a short time it would have returned to its former state. The greenhouse gases were essential to our plan, but they were not enough in themselves. Our message was simple: if it is to sustain life, an environment must contain life.

All we did was help things along with a bit of Gaian manipulation, but that was only a start, and we knew it.

Millions of miles from Earth, in an environment that was still barely tolerable and with radiation levels much higher than those on Earth (although as soon as we began adding oxygen to the atmosphere an ozone layer formed to provide protection against ultraviolet radiation), evolution worked fairly rapidly (mainly so its first manifestations might emerge within the timespan of our story). Species began to differ from the ancestral forms conveyed from Earth. Mars had been made Earthlike, but from then on it would diverge to follow its own evolutionary paths.

We did our best to check our science and although we played one or two games and, just for fun, invented one or two somewhat dubious devices, so far as possible the Mars with which we dealt was the real Mars. As I said, it checked out when the central idea was tested. The book was written in a lighthearted style, but beneath the surface we were perfectly serious.

COLONIES AWAY FROM EARTH

Public and governmental enthusiasm for space ventures waxes and wanes almost as regularly as the Moon. Our book was launched at a low point, when people were looking in the other direction, but since then interest has begun to revive and there is talk now of manned explorations of Mars and of Martian colonies that would need to be self-sustaining because Mars is so far away. Someone has said that a century from now there will be 100,000 people living on Mars.

Many of the plans are visionary in that they underestimate the biological difficulties of living away from Earth. Everyone accepts that colonists would need to produce their own food and the simplest way is to grow it, and that wastes would need processing, nutrients and gases cycling and so forth, but what no one has yet discovered is how small and simple the necessary community of organisms can be that will fulfil these functions and remain fully self-sustaining. Laboratory attempts to construct such microcosms usually fail.

Nevertheless, the plans go on being made and some go much further than Mars, into the outer reaches of the solar system and then beyond, across the galaxy. Scientists have calculated how long it should take for humans, or their descendants, to colonise every potentially habitable planet in the Milky Way.

Is star travel possible? Provided you do not imagine anything can travel faster than the speed of light, why not? Establish a colony from Earth on a vehicle in such a way that it can survive there for many generations, gently accelerate the vehicle away from the solar system, and eventually it will arrive in the vicinity of another star. The original migrants will be long dead, of course, and it will be their descendants who arrive, centuries or even thousands of years later, but theoretically it should be possible one day.

Humans have an impressive record of overcoming difficulties, especially those of their own devising, and there are many people who believe it inevitable that humans will travel to other planets and then live on them. The question is not whether this will happen but merely how soon.

Why would anyone want to embark on such a voyage? Jim and I had to find an answer to that for our book. It did not take us long, for it has been answered already, many times. Why did Polynesians set out across the Pacific in flimsy boats, with no certainty of ever finding land? Why did Europeans flock to the New World, to Australia, to any of the countless other places they colonised? They travelled, at great risk and into what was then the unknown, because that is what humans do. It is as simple, or complex, as that.

A PASSION FOR INFORMATION

Now let us put together a few observations. All animals learn by doing, by practice, and all of them learn from their mistakes. Most animals can communicate to others what they themselves have learned. At the simplest level this happens when the young learn by imitating the behaviour of the adults they see around them, and it also means animals can communicate what they have learned to their own offspring. Thus several characteristics we may like to think of as uniquely human in fact are commonplace.

There is a quantitative difference, however, so large that it has developed into a qualitative difference. Humans can communicate much more than any other species; we can communicate abstract concepts that can be expressed only in language and never by practical demonstration; and we can communicate not only from one generation to the next but by leaping across many generations. You and I can read books that were written many centuries ago, receiving information directly, without intermediaries, from a person long dead. What is more, humans have an insatiable appetite for information and ideas, for communicating them, and for storing them like misers.

That is my first observation. The second is related to it and concerns our curiosity. We seek information actively, and have no hesitation in travelling to wherever it may be obtained. This makes us into explorers, and we have always been explorers. Our explorations now are taking us away from our own planet. It seems obvious that colonies will be established away from Earth for the simple reason that we have imagined and willed that this be so, and that the dream be made to come true the very moment its realisation is technologically feasible.

We will leave Earth, but what will we do then? If we wish to survive we will build for ourselves environments that mimic that of Earth, the only environment in which we can live. We will have to construct such environments inside vehicles we have made or, when opportunity affords, on other suitable planets. Each of these new environments, together with its inhabitants, will start at once to evolve in its own way, but however remote it may be in space or time, appearance or composition, it will always be possible to trace its ancestry to Earth.

IS GAIA ABOUT TO REPRODUCE?

Let us now return to the Gaian idea. The Earth, I have said, is in effect a single living organism. Imagine you are a biologist studying some entirely novel organism no one has seen before. You watch it regulating its own functions but perhaps with more difficulty as it grows older. Then, after it has been in existence for quite a long time, although you cannot know in advance how long such an organism may be expected to live, something new happens. Among all its organs (on Earth the particular groups of organisms that deal with particular functions) a new type appears, composed of individual units and groups of units.

At first this new organ seems to have no particular function but as you continue to watch it you realise what it is doing. The individual units multiply rapidly, soon colonising every part of the organism, and wherever they go they collect information about the organism of which they are part. They seem to specialise, some collecting information of one kind, some of another. All this information is cherished, stored and transmitted enthusiastically from individual to individual, generation to generation, and as time goes on the information stores grow ever larger.

After a time, and not a very long time when measured against the age of the total organism, these individuals and groups start to leave, taking their information with them. They travel, in capsules of various sizes, first a short way from the organism, then a little further, until they have gained enough confidence to embark on the building of small-scale duplicates of the organism from which they came.

As a biologist, what would you make of all this? It seems to me that only one explanation makes sense. The little capsules containing individuals flying away in all directions are the equivalent of seeds or spores, some kind of reproductive structure. The organism is reproducing, and this is its method.

Are the little individuals intelligent? It all depends on

what you mean by intelligent, another word that is still hunting for a satisfactory definition although we all think we know what it means. Obviously they must be able to deal efficiently with large amounts of information. Equally obviously they must be very ingenious, for they have built their own capsules and when they arrive wherever it is they are going they will need to work fast if they are to make conditions tolerable for themselves, before the living communities they carry to sustain them start to fail. If this adds up to something you can call intelligence, then they are intelligent.

So far as anyone knows, the Earth is quite alone. If there are other planets that support life they are very far away and there is no communication with them. If the Earth is reproducing itself, therefore, it is doing so asexually. This is quite usual, however. Asexual reproduction occurs in many species and especially among the prokaryotes on which the Earth relies so heavily. There is no reason why the large organism should not employ a similar method, and were it to do so this is what it might look like. Tiny versions of itself (our space capsules and ships) carrying enough information to grow new copies of the original would fly away in search of places they found or could make habitable.

I hope this does not depress you. It is intended only to find for us humans the role we would so dearly like to have, and it is a perfectly respectable, indeed honourable role. It makes no sense to think of ourselves as the brains of the planet, or its conscience or moral sense, so how can we find some kind of cosmic use for talents that really are uniquely human? At least my suggestion accords with what we can observe. Humans may not be 'seeds of the Earth', but we are behaving as though we were, so it comes to the same thing in the end.

MISTAKING THE FINGER FOR THE MOON

Does this reintroduce the teleological difficulty? I think not. It would be teleological to propose that human evolution is directed toward a goal beyond ourselves, but it is not teleological to describe the development of an embryo to a fetus to an infant to a child to an adult, even though the outcome is known to us from the start. That is simply a process involving a series of identifiable stages, and in likening the planet to a single organism that is all I am doing, describing a developmental process that at one stage includes humans. The difference is that in this case some of the constituent parts are also evolving independently within the whole organism. I say nothing about the future evolution of humans or anything else, except that it is likely to continue for some time yet and I see no reason to suppose we have reached its end. There is no further goal towards which evolution is directed, so far as I am aware, beyond that of surviving.

In any case, I have another point to make, or more precisely a point I have made repeatedly, but now expressed a little differently. Gaia is not a person; it is a metaphor, and it would be unwise to believe in it too literally. As this example demonstrates, when you take the metaphor too far the strain begins to show. Gaia may be an organism, but is it one whose constituent parts are pursuing evolutionary paths of their own, separately from the whole, as though within your body your liver were slowly turning into something else?

To call an idea a metaphor is not to diminish it. Warning against the worship of individuals, Buddhists point out that Buddhas show the way. They are like fingers pointing at the Moon, and we should beware of mistaking the finger for the Moon. We live and think by metaphors and they are extremely useful. It helps to relate something unfamiliar or difficult to understand to something else that is simpler and very familiar.

Never mind for the moment whether or not the Earth really is a single living organism. Just assume, provisionally if you like, that in many respects it is very like one. This allows us to study its component parts in relation to one another and to the whole, as though they were organs in a body, and if we can do that perhaps we can also examine planetary disorders as though they were diseases. As we deal with the alarming array of environmental problems presented to us almost daily, this could be very helpful indeed.

12
PHYSICIANS TO A PLANET

The purpose of science, as an activity, is to observe natural phenomena, devise explanations to account for them, and then to test those explanations, usually by experiment. At any rate, this is what is supposed to happen, even if it is not always the way things work out. The point is that, although scientists strive always to reveal the truth, scientific theories and hypotheses are not in themselves statements of an absolute truth. They are best guesses that may be modified or even abandoned in the light of subsequent observations or because they fail when tested.

A theory is not the same thing as an hypothesis. A theory is a fairly rigorous explanation based on observation, and usually it is quite robust because it has been developed over a long time. An hypothesis is less robust. It is a kind of offer of an explanation, an idea that can be defended by logical argument but that only time, much more observation and experimental testing can convert into a theory .

Theories are approximations to the truth, but they are also tools. They allow predictions to be made and this means account can be taken of them in the planning of other experiments to test other proposals or, indeed, in enterprises of many kinds. The theory of gravity, for example, describes not merely the fact that bodies attract one another but the values that can be attached to this attractive force in respect of different kinds and sizes of bodies and under different circumstances. Architects, civil engineers and space technologists are among those who use the theory every day. They need not question whether or not it is true. The important thing is that it works, that calculations based on it are reliable, and this means that buildings, bridges and orbiting satellites stay where they are put.

THREATS TO THE ENVIRONMENT

The Gaian proposal is an hypothesis. It is offered as an explanation. There is some evidence to support it and it can be defended logically, but it has not yet accumulated sufficient observational and experimental support for it to be described as a theory. Meanwhile, there is nothing wrong in treating it as though it were a theory and seeing what happens. We are entitled to ask whether it can be used to help in making predictions and, if so, what sort of predictions.

It describes the Earth or, to put it another way, the natural environment, and these days the natural environment is the subject of a great deal of attention. Environmental concern is not new in itself. In the first century AD Lucius Columella, a soldier and landowner, wrote 12 books called *De Re Rustica* (Of Things Rural) in which he criticised the slave-based industrialisation of Roman agriculture by absentee landlords and its effects on the soil. In medieval England laws were passed to prevent deforestation and to restrict the burning of coal because of the pollution it caused. There are many organisations, some of them founded in the last century, dedicated to the conservation of wildlife and the protection of landscapes and buildings.

The new concern, which began in the early 1960s following the publication of Rachel Carson's *Silent Spring*, is different, however. There is a good deal of overlap but essentially the modern environmental movement is distinct from the older conservation movement. Environmentalists worry about threats to the planet as a whole, about the possibility that human activities may disrupt processes of which we know little, with long-term consequences that may be catastrophic.

By their persistent campaigning and clever use of

publicity, environmentalists have made the physical and biological welfare of the planet into an issue politicians cannot ignore. For this we owe them a debt of gratitude, but in order to achieve this level of public awareness they have had to make themselves heard above the incessant clamour of daily news and entertainment. A story will not make prime-time television unless it is dramatic, and if it describes a problem it must come complete with an instant solution. This may be a criticism of modern journalism; it is not a criticism of environmentalists who had no choice in how to present their case. All the same, the sensationalisation of issues and their associated solutions creates a difficulty. How are we to evaluate them?

CLASSIFYING PROBLEMS

This is where the Gaian idea can help. It allows us to examine each issue in the light of its possible effects on the operation of the system that is the planet. Will it interfere with mechanisms of self-regulation? If it does, how may the planet seek to restore the balance? If the balance cannot be restored what are the likely consequences and when may we expect them to appear?

An approach along these lines can lead to a system of classification for environmental problems. We can say, for example, that the hunting and killing of whales is unlikely to have any serious effect on the planet as a whole. Whales have always been too few in number to have much influence. The Gaian consequences of whaling are trivial.

This does not mean the issue itself is trivial and far less does it mean an activity, in this case whaling, should continue. The categorisation means no more than it says and it would be a serious mistake to read more into it or to pretend that this is the only way to evaluate issues or that Gaian issues are the only ones that should concern us.

It may mean, for example, that the underlying concern is primarily moral or ethical rather than scientific. I believe whaling is wrong because I do not believe humans have the right or need to kill whales. I know some people eat whalemeat and that a few subsistence economies may be based on whaling, but there are alternatives. The number of people involved is small and there are alternative foods and could be alternative ways of life. It seems to me that proposing an end to whaling is not the same as proposing to end the raising of farm animals for food.

This is an ethical argument and if someone could prove conclusively that whaling cannot possibly bring about the extinction of any species of whales I would not change my view. I maintain it is absolutely wrong to kill a single whale. Recognising that this is the true basis for my view, I accept that surveys of whale populations, studies of breeding and feeding habits and of the behaviour and social arrangements of whales are valuable, but I do not accept that they have any relevance whatever to the morality of whaling. Were they to reveal that whales have unsavoury habits and are really ugly, unpleasant animals I would still maintain we have no right to kill them.

A second category might include problems that are purely local. The disposal of toxic industrial wastes might fit into this category. Such wastes exist and something must be done with them, but it must be done in such a way as to ensure they do not introduce harmful contaminants into the immediate environment. Clearly, disposal requires regulation on a global scale because these days wastes are traded internationally, but the problems caused by careless disposal are always local. If they have Gaian consequences these are unlikely to be serious.

Then there are regional problems, which are somewhat more serious from a Gaian point of view. These might include the discharge of wastes, not especially toxic in themselves, into rivers that discharge into shallow, more or less landlocked seas where they may accumulate to harmful concentrations. The European rivers that carry wastes into the North, Baltic and Mediterranean Seas are good examples. Such pollution may cause a Gaian type of damage in those seas, but it is unlikely to have wider consequences. Nevertheless it amounts to a Gaian problem, if a minor one. Again, I must point out that in describing it as minor I do not mean it should be ignored or that steps to deal with it may be postponed.

Finally we reach the highest or most serious category of all, comprising those activities that may affect the overall welfare of the planet. This is the category that produces surprises. There are serious problems that are not usually thought of as problems at all, apparent problems that turn out to be minor or even trivial, and problems whose causes turn out to be very different from those which most of us supposed.

GEOPHYSIOLOGY AND GEOPHYSICIANS

This way of dealing with problems has a close parallel that becomes evident if you change the word 'problem' to 'symptom'. We are approaching the planet in much the same way that a physician approaches a patient. For this reason, Jim Lovelock has proposed that the scientific discipline dedicated to studying the Earth in this way be called geophysiology. The scientists who collect information that helps them understand the 'organs' by which the planet regulates itself and the relationships of one 'organ' to another would thus be called geophysiologists and, as with medical students, this version of physiology would form an integral part of the training for practitioners of the ultimate discipline, the geophysicians, the healers of the Earth. People often say the Earth is sick and wish it might be restored to health. This terminology takes the metaphor at its face value. The parallel is quite close, after all.

It may be coincidence, but there is even more behind the medical analogy than there seems. In ancient Greece the centre of the flat Earth was believed to be at Delphi, where there was also the most famous of all oracles. Those who wished to understand the world, and especially what effect it might have on them, consulted the oracle. The oracle itself was below ground. Originally it emanated from the Earth, Gaia, manifested in the form of the serpent Python, usually regarded as male, who communicated to a priestess, the Pythia. According to one legend, the oracle passed from Gaia to her daughter Themis and thence to Phoebe, who gave it to Apollo as a birthday present. The alternative legend holds that Apollo killed the serpent and took over the oracle. In either case Apollo became the resident god and it was he whom visitors consulted.

Apollo had many aspects. He was associated with music, poetry and dance, was the war god of Troy, could bring plagues on those who offended him, but most of all he concerned himself with protecting crops and livestock from harm and through that with protecting all natural things. It was to Apollo that Hippocrates dedicated his oath, or code of conduct, for physicians. I have no idea whether doctors actually swear the Hippocratic oath these days and if they do I expect the dedication to Apollo has been deleted, but if they do, whether they know it or not, he is the god they are addressing. The link is clear between knowledge of and care for the Earth and natural things, and health.

THREATS TO GAIA

This approach helps immediately with issues related to environmental pollution. Pollutants are poisons so far as the natural environment is concerned, so we can regard pollution in the same way that we regard the poisoning of humans or other animals.

Poisons vary widely in their potency. This means the dose that can cause injury or death varies from one poison to another, and the size of a dose must be measured in relation to the size of the body receiving it. It takes a very much larger dose of cyanide than a modern nerve gas to kill a person, for example, and most poisonous substances are harmless in very small doses. At the same time, what would be a small dose for a human would be a very large dose for a mouse; thus the risk posed by a poison depends on the relationship between the size of the dose and the body size of the victim.

The same is true of environmental pollutants, whose harmful effects can be calculated at a local, regional or global level. A small discharge of a noxious substance may kill everything that lives in a small lake, the inhabitants of a very large lake can survive a much bigger dose, and the dose required to kill the inhabitants of the open oceans is so large it is difficult to see how humans could possibly produce or administer it. It is possible to assert quite confidently that our industrial activities may cause serious injury locally to lakes, or regionally to landlocked seas, but that they present no threat to the open oceans.

DESTABILISING THE CLIMATE

Our knowledge of the Earth is still rudimentary, but already a Gaian interpretation of climate regulation throws considerable light on the possible consequences of our burning of carbon-based fuels. We are releasing carbon dioxide. This is not the only gas that contributes to the greenhouse warming of the planet, but it is the one we are injecting into the atmosphere in the largest amount.

Carbon dioxide is also released as a consequence of deforestation in the tropics, and so this must be checked. Poor people who need land to grow food and wood for fuel must be provided with alternative ways to live, and the large corporations that invest in deforestation must be prevented from so doing. This will lead to more expensive forms of aid to tropical countries and to reduced corporate profits, but the price is worth paying when you consider the alternative.

A description of signs and symptoms leads to a diagnosis and prognosis and thence to the prescription of a remedy. The remedy in this case may not be popular but medicines are not expected to be pleasant.

If we are to avoid, or at least limit, the climatic effects of our activities, we must reduce very substantially the amount of carbon dioxide we release into the air, which implies that we will have to learn to rely very much less on the burning of wood, peat, coal, oil and natural gas — the carbon-based fuels. Clearly, we must find alternative sources of energy.

Energy conservation measures will help, of course, but they are difficult, and not necessarily cheap, to implement.

The so-called renewable sources of energy can, and must, play a part and should be developed, but their contribution is necessarily limited. Passive solar heat, based on solar collectors, can provide useful amounts of water heating, and some space heating, but it is of limited value in cool, wet climates. Solar cells, converting sunlight directly into electricity, may also be useful for supplying power to buildings, although it is doubtful whether they will supply enough for most industrial processes. The growing of crops as a source of fuel is inappropriate, of course, since the fuel in question is carbon.

Wind, wave and tides will also have a part to play, but again the possibilities for their use are limited. Wind generators are very useful for supplying remote communities, for whom they can sometimes prove cheaper than a link to a distant grid line, but as soon as you imagine them providing more than a very small proportion of the electric power needed by a nation, environmental problems arise. The windmills take up a great deal of space. There are wind farms, for example, in parts of the USA, but it is difficult to picture them in crowded Europe.

If you allow that each wind generator is rated at around one megawatt output, at least one thousand are required to match the output from a modern conventional power station. The generators must be spaced at some distance from one another to prevent them interfering with each other's airflow. In practice, they occupy about three acres each. So, to match a conventional power station a wind farm is likely to require some 3,000 acres (about 1,200 hectares). They must be sited in windy places, on high ground, coastal cliffs and offshore islands, but in Britain, for example, these are usually places of great scenic beauty and jealously guarded against industrial development. The generators require buildings to house ancillary equipment and the power they produce must be fed into a supply, so they must be accompanied by overhead power lines and pylons.

Quite apart from the visual intrusion, a wind farm site would have to be closed to the public because of the dangers arising from high-voltage power lines and the risk that a turbine might fail. Wind generators are no safer than any other generating source. They are also extremely noisy.

Various devices have been designed to harness the movement of sea waves. Obviously, these are of use only to countries that have coastlines, and the number of suitable sites is limited. Similarly, there are not many coastal areas where the tidal movement is large enough to be harnessed, and the necessary barrages (dams) are likely to cause severe ecological disturbance by altering the flow of water and deposition of silt.

The only alternative that really can provide the amount of energy we need is nuclear power. This is too expensive for many of the poorer countries at their present stage of economic development but if the richer countries adopt it as their principal source of energy, poorer countries can continue to burn carbon-based fuel, and this will still represent a substantial global reduction in the use of carbon.

Environmentalist opposition to nuclear power will make this difficult, but attitudes can change. Unless they do change, such obstruction may be directly responsible for by far the most serious environmental catastrophe threatening us. This opposition is based on a quite irrational fear of the process and products of radioactive decay. Exposure to high levels of radiation is harmful, certainly, but all of us are exposed to low levels all our lives, the largest single source being the food we eat. We are radioactive and our species, indeed all life, evolved in a radioactive environment. This makes it very unlikely that there is not a safety margin allowing us to be exposed without harm to radiation levels somewhat above a background average, calculated in any case as the average of levels that vary widely from one place to another. Even counting Chernobyl, emissions from the nuclear industry are relatively small. In Gaian terms the dangers of nuclear power fall into the category of non-problems, while those of burning fossil fuels are planet-endangering.

Apart from worries about the safety of reactors while they are in operation, people are concerned about radioactive wastes, some of which must be isolated from the environment for a very long time. Again, the scale of the problem has been exaggerated. Nuclear wastes are classified according to the amount and type of radiation they emit, as low, medium, and high level. Low-level waste consists of material that is barely radioactive at all — overalls, gloves, laboratory equipment and other such items, many of them from hospitals and research laboratories with no connection with power generation. They can disposed of safely without difficulty, by landfill burial for example.

High-level waste, consisting of reactor fuel rods as they are removed from reactors, is hot (literally) and intensely radioactive. It is stored in ponds, under water, for some years, until it has cooled and has lost much of its radioactivity, and so becomes medium-level waste.

In Britain, until now, medium-level waste has remained in storage, but in the next decade or so it will have to be moved. The plan is to process the waste to make it into cylindrical blocks of a solid, glass-like substance. Each block will then be sealed in a container designed to absorb most of the radiation. In this form the waste will be placed in a well-ventilated store so the flow of air continues to cool it. Depending on the composition of the waste it will remain in the store for about 50 years. Then it will be no warmer than its surroundings, most of its radioactivity will have gone, and it will be moved to a permanent store, probably below ground, where it must remain isolated for several centuries, perhaps for as long as a thousand years. This is a long time, but the store can be sealed securely as soon as it is full, it requires no supervision or management, and were anyone to break in the waste would not harm them unless they remained very close to it for many hours.

Is this dangerous? The British have been storing reactor waste for more than a quarter of a century and there have been no accidental releases of radioactive waste substances so far, nor of civil reactor waste anywhere in the world. The problems of disposal are well known and understood.

When a reactor reaches the end of its useful life, it must be decommissioned. This operation, too, has been planned carefully, and the cost of it allowed for in pricing policy. When the buildings have been demolished, what is left of the reactor itself remains sealed inside a kind of bunker. In most cases other reactors will have replaced it on the same site, so it will be just one concrete building among many.

There is more anti-greenhouse medicine yet. Methane is also implicated. Its concentration is growing because of an increase in wet rice cultivation and the farming of ruminants, mainly cattle. We cannot advise a reduction in rice growing, because this supplies a staple food to many people, so we should accept that a diet containing less beef and dairy produce would not harm us, and reduce cattle farming substantially. We should also restrict severely the use of chlorofluorocarbons, which are much more effective than carbon dioxide as greenhouse gases.

THE OZONE LAYER

Chlorofluorocarbons (CFCs) have achieved notoriety principally by being implicated in the depletion of the ozone layer. This has been represented as a major environmental problem, but is it? And is it a Gaian problem?

An ordinary oxygen molecule consists of two atoms (O_2). When sufficient energy is applied to the molecule its atoms can separate and then reform in threes. The three-atom molecule, O_3, is ozone. At altitudes between about 10 and 50 kilometres (33,000 to 164,000 feet) but most intensely around 20 kilometres (66,000 feet) ultraviolet radiation, the portion of sunlight that is just beyond the violet end of the visible light spectrum, has enough energy to produce this effect. Oxygen molecules are split, reform as ozone, the ozone is split, and so the process continues. Apart from producing ozone, the reaction absorbs ultraviolet radiation. Were there significantly less ozone being formed and reformed, and were there no other atmospheric absorbant, more ultraviolet radiation would reach the ground surface.

The first fears about depletion of the ozone layer were voiced around 1970, when the threat was deemed likely to come from nitrogen oxides in the exhaust fumes of fleets of passenger transport aircraft that would be flying at these high altitudes. The aircraft would fly at supersonic speeds, but this was irrelevant: it was the altitude that mattered. The transport fleets were never built, in modest amounts nitrogen oxides were found to increase ozone production rather than reduce it, and for a time the danger receded. It subsequently re-emerged on several occasions, due, for example, to nitrogen compounds originating in agricultural fertilisers, and finally with CFCs. More recently it was discovered that in the very strange atmospheric conditions that prevail over Antarctica the ozone layer there is being depleted at certain times of the year, and chlorine is involved in the chemical reactions responsible.

CFCs are highly stable compounds. This means that once in the air they do not break down readily and some are carried into the stratosphere where they do decompose, chlorine being one of the decomposition products. Thus CFCs are taken to be the source of the chlorine (although methyl chloride emitted by plankton may be a larger source).

A Gaian threat arises only if three conditions are fulfilled: the Antarctic ozone depletion must spread to lower, populated latitudes; the depletion must lead to increased surface exposure to ultraviolet radiation; and that exposure must be harmful.

High above the South Pole air temperatures are much lower than they are at similar altitudes anywhere else, the air is much drier, and as the Antarctic winter draws to an end air movements around the Pole create vortices of a type and on a scale not known elsewhere. It is under these conditions that depletion occurs and it is by no means certain that it can spread much beyond the Antarctic continent itself, although a similar but smaller ozone hole may occur over the North Pole.

A depletion of the ozone layer does not necessarily lead to increased surface exposure to ultraviolet radiation, though. Ozone may form at other levels and, although it may not form a distinct layer in the atmosphere, what matters is the total ozone column, the total amount of the gas through which light must pass between the top of the atmosphere and the ground. Over much of the world, and perhaps everywhere, the total ozone column is fairly steady or increasing, which compensates for any loss at high altitude.

Nor is ozone the only absorber of ultraviolet radiation. High altitude haze also absorbs it and this haze has increased in recent years. I mentioned earlier that skies are less intensely blue than they were when I was a child. This is the reason. The haze is due mainly to increased activity by phytoplankton and, because of its added absorption, the amount of ultraviolet radiation reaching the ground is tending to decrease.

The formation of ozone depends on the intensity of sunlight, and this varies greatly from place to place and season to season. Consequently the thickness of the ozone layer is subject to great variability. In summer, when there are many hours of daylight, it is very high in middle and high latitudes, but it thins as the days grow shorter and almost disappears in polar regions during their dark winter. Generally, it is thinner in equatorial regions than it is most of the time further from the equator. The ozone may be several times thicker in one place than in another. Yet living organisms seem not to be affected. The belief that ultraviolet radiation is harmful may be based on experiments in which bacteria are killed when exposed to it. Such bacteria are obtained from cultures in which they grow without the protective coating that in natural conditions all bacterial colonies always have. Such coated bacteria are not harmed by ultraviolet, which is only weakly penetrative, and marine organisms are protected either by being below the maximum level of sea water to which ultraviolet light can penetrate, or by the presence in the water of chemical compounds that react when this energy is applied to them, so absorbing the radiation.

It is true that some skin cancers in fair-skinned people are caused by excessive exposure to ultraviolet radiation and that these have become more prevalent in recent years. This is not due to any increase in the amount of ultraviolet radiation reaching the surface, because as I pointed out this has decreased, not increased. It is more likely to be due to the fashion for prolonged sunbathing, especially by those who travel from their high latitude homes to lower latitudes for that express purpose.

Studies of the region of the atmosphere in which the ozone layer occurs are important because they provide information relevant to studies of the global climate. Depletion of the layer is unlikely to be very harmful and it presents no planet-endangering threat in a Gaian sense.

ACID RAIN

Ozone is a very reactive gas with a pungent smell. It is formed by electric sparks, which supply the necessary energy, and if you are close to the spark you can smell it. It is a respiratory irritant that will set you coughing if you inhale even a small amount. Inhale much more and it will kill you. In strong sunlight it is also produced near the ground by reactions involving vehicle exhausts, a pollutant implicated in acid rain, another environmental issue it is helpful to examine from a Gaian point of view.

All rainfall is slightly acid because it contains small amounts of such substances as dissolved carbon dioxide (carbonic acid), nitrogen oxides (nitric acid) and sulphates (sulphuric acid). Acid rain is precipitation in which the acidity is markedly greater than usual. The word 'rain' is misleading, for acid precipitation is most damaging when dry particles are deposited on plants directly and then dissolved in dew, or when an acidic mist or fog blankets vegetation. In contrast, rain usually washes away fairly quickly.

The first report of acid rain was more than a century ago, so the phenomenon is not new. In 1852 R.A. Smith presented to the Manchester Literary and Philosophical Society a paper called 'On the air and rain of Manchester' in which he reported the presence of sulphuric acid in rainfall, with its concentration increasing the closer the sampling points were to the city. It had caused extensive damage to limestone buildings in many continental European cities as well as Manchester, and was recognised as a matter requiring remedial action. Monitoring began in southern England in 1853, although acid rain was not detected until many years later. By 1913 it had been detected and was being measured over industrial northern England.

Modern reports began in the early 1970s, in Scandinavia, then in Germany and other parts of central Europe and in eastern North America. Industry was blamed, and in particular coal-fired power plants, especially in Britain and the US. But there was more to it than met the eye. In both countries gaseous emissions of sulphur and nitrogen compounds had been decreasing for years, and it seemed an odd time for problems to emerge. Many acid-damaged buildings had been restored and showed no sign of recent damage, always the most immediate indication of air pollution by sulphur. Finally, German forests supported an abundance of lichens that are very intolerant of sulphur, and analyses showed the forest air to be remarkably free from that pollutant. In southern Scandinavia, on the other hand, soils were found to contain high levels of sulphur compounds.

After years of investigation it became clear there is no single acid rain phenomenon to account for all the observations. In Scandinavia, the northeast United States and southeast Canada damage is caused by airborne sulphur compounds falling on soils and draining into lakes. Trees may be damaged and if the soils contain little calcium a series of reactions may occur that release aluminium compounds into the water, and these compounds are injurious to fish. The sulphur is not necessarily harmful in itself; indeed, some sulphur-enriched lakes are made more biologically productive and contain more fish. So far as the sulphur is an industrial pollutant, in Scandinavia most comes from Sweden, the USSR, Poland, Czechloslovakia and East Germany, with some from Britain, but the biggest source, almost certainly, is not industrial at all but DMS (dimethyl sulphide) released by marine plankton. The DMS release appears to be linked to the greenhouse climatic warning. In central Europe a combination of drought in 1976, disease and local pollution, mainly by nitrogen oxides and ozone from vehicle exhausts, are the cause of damage to trees.

From a Gaian point of view, acid rain causes little harm and is not a serious problem. This is not to say it does not matter. The livelihoods of those who depend on forestry and freshwater fishing are at stake, so if the situation can be remedied, obviously it should be. The remedy is not simple, however, although a convenient medicine may be available. Agricultural lime is cheap, plentiful and supplies calcium to reduce acidity and inhibit the reactions that release aluminium. It is not a cure, but sometimes the best of doctors are reduced to treating only the symptoms of a particularly intractable complaint. At least it stops the pain.

The acid rain phenomenon is one of those that illustrate the dangers of hasty diagnosis and instant prescription. It is easier than you think to jump to a conclusion that seems obvious but is wrong, and mistakes are usually expensive. Fitting flue-gas desulphurisation units to existing power plants will cost a great deal, for example, but their effect on acid rain damage will be slight and they will cause Gaia harm in other ways. They use lime (calcium hydroxide) to react with the flue gases to form gypsum (calcium sulphate). The lime is obtained by mining limestone (calcium carbonate) and heating it in kilns to drive off the carbon dioxide, leaving quicklime (calcium oxide) that is slaked by the addition of water to make the hydroxide. In Britain alone desulphurisation is planned to use several hundreds of thousands of tons of limestone a year and the carbon dioxide released during kilning may be more harmful than the sulphur.

ENVIRONMENTAL HYPOCHONDRIA

There are other environmental problems, ephemeral in that they emerge, are debated briefly, and then vanish when they are shown to be wholly imaginary. At one time there were fears that tropical deforestation would alter the carbon cycle in such a way as to deplete the atmosphere of its oxygen. We would all asphyxiate. Such fears now seem foolish, but then, the imagined illnesses of hypochondriacs also seem foolish to those who lack the perception to see they mask a deeper and genuine malaise. The hypochondriac may well be sick, but not from the imagined disease. Clearing vast tracts of tropical forest will not destroy the oxygen in the air, but that does not mean it is safe to do so, that no harm may result. Tropical forests appear to play a critical role in global climate regulation, but it is only recently that this has come to be suspected. The hypochondria masks a real and warranted concern, and what is true for this manifestation is probably true for others.

There are other problems that so far have received little or no popular attention but of which we may hear more in the next year or two. There has been concern, for example, about the contamination of water by nitrates from fertilisers. The health risks of this contamination have been greatly exaggerated. Babies can be harmed, but instances are extremely rare, and there is no convincing evidence that nitrates can harm adults. This is another case of hypochondria and it, too, masks what may be a genuine malady.

Worldwide, the amount of nitrogen compounds polluting groundwater, calculated as nitrous oxide (N_2O), has been estimated as between 800,000 and 1,700,000 tons a year. The amount produced in the atmosphere naturally is about 8,800,000 tons a year so human activity is adding amounts equal to 10 to 20 per cent of the natural amount. This estimate, which assumes only 1 per cent of the world's groundwater to be contaminated, is likely to be conservative. I outlined earlier the way organisms regulate the cycling of nitrogen. It might be wise to consider the extent to which we are perturbing the cycle and to try to predict the possible consequences.

A GAIAN FUTURE

Left to itself, the planet would have no need of healing, at least no healing that we might supply. Once trained, the geophysicians will be concerned with ailments caused by our own activities. They will offer diagnoses and treatments, of course, but as the years pass and they acquire greater experience and confidence we must hope they will come to devote most of their time to a global preventive medicine. They will be able to predict the outcome of proposed innovations and this will make their contributions vital to all planning processes.

They will be the specialists. More generally, the Gaian hypothesis promises to bring together two great branches of the scientific enterprise, the Earth sciences and the life sciences, in a unified description of the way our planet functions. The fruits of that unification will be intellectually satisfying but also of great practical value, for the understanding they bring will allow us to live in greater harmony with other species than is possible today.

Indeed, the hypothesis will touch our lives at many levels. It arises from a mythology thousands of years old that occurs, with variations in the terminology used, in many cultures in many parts of the world. It challenges our perception not only of the Earth but of ourselves as inhabitants of the Earth. At this level it speaks to us all, through our literature and religious beliefs and experiences, and it is relevant to the way we arrange our political and social institutions, as in the emphasis it places on the importance of collaboration and the dangers of competition.

Our ancestors were members of tribes whose horizons extended no further than the boundaries within which they obtained their food. As time passed and tribes united to form nations the boundaries widened, and in a few places nations united within an entire continent. We are still confined, some of us more than others, by our memories of such antique boundaries, but all of them are obsolete. Gradually we are being forced to regard the world as a single entity. Our outlook is becoming less parochial. The Gaian idea defines the global horizons within which we now live.

INDEX

acid rain, 78, 139, 170-173
acidity, 96
Adriatic, 67
Aegean Sea, 67
air, 49, 50
air bubbles, 50
air pressure, 42
albedo, 149
algae, 75
aliens, 20
Alps, 93
altitudes, 22-23
Anaxagorus, 17
animals: 86, 100-104; analysis
    of, 81; building walls, 68-70
Antarctic, 137, 168
Antarctica, 49-50
Arctic, 124
Arrhenius, Svante August, 48
asexual reproduction, 154
asteroid belt, 24
Athenagorus, 5
Atlantic, 67
atmosphere: climate change, 50;
    looking for life, 22-23, 24-26,
    34, 38, 39; Mars, 148;
    original, on Earth, 53;
    pollution, 41, 136, 163; see
    also carbon dioxide, nitrogen,
    oxygen
Atmospheric Environment
    Service, 137
Axelrod, Robert, 117
Aztecs, 9

bacteria, 34, 37, 38, 41, 84, 91,
    105-107, 108, 130, 138, 169
basalt, 56
'big bang', 29
biological world, 86-87
Black Sea, 67
body fluids, 63
body tissues, 76
Bosporus, 67
Buddha, 155

carbon, 37, 51-54, 55, 78, 83, 91,
    138
carbon cycle, 54, 129
carbon dioxide, 51, 131, 139;
    amount in atmosphere, 136
cattle, 167
causes and effects, 115
cells, 61, 63, 147
cells, simple and complex,
    108-109
Challenger, F., 80
chemistry, 21, 22
chlorine, 38, 59, 82
chlorofluorocarbons (CFCs), 38,
    136, 167
chlorophyll, 36
climate, 11, 43, 97, 122, 128, 129,
    135, 141; destabilising the,
    163-167; global, 170
Coleridge, Samuel Taylor, 61
collaboration of organisms,
    116-117
comets, 33
communities, 104; global,
    109-110
competition, 123;
    biological, 103
complexity, 124-125
computer simulations, 148
continental drift, 92-94
coral reefs, 68, 70
corals, 69
Crawford, Peter, 102
Cretaceous period, 50

daisyworlds, 120-124
Dardanelles, 67
Darwin, Charles, 88-90, 98, 99,
    100, 102
Darwinism, 88-90, 109
Dead Sea, 58, 60, 66
decomposers, 52
deforestation, 163, 173
Delphi, oracle of, 161
Dévai, István, 82

dimethyl sulphide (DMS), 138, 139, 172
drainage, 66
drought, 137

Earth: assaults on, 132-133; atmosphere, 25-26; carbon cycle, 54, 129; fevered?, 135-137; Gaian description of, 158; injuring the, 146; inner core, 32; life altered chemistry of, 27; lifeless, 53; living, 9-13; Mother, 4-6, 8-9; oceans, 56-57; radioactive, 47; as a robust planet, 134; sciences, 8, 174; as a sick planet, 11-12, 161; *see also* Gaia
ecology, 89
elements, 46
energy conservation, 164
energy, from stars, 23
environment: vii, 11, 131; awareness of, 88; classifying problems, 159-161; and hypochondria, 173; influenced by living beings, 92; pollution of, 41, 131, 136, 158-159, 162-163; symptoms of illness, 12; warnings to, 87
environmental changes, 86, 106
environmental regulation, 123
estuaries, 64
eukaryotes, 108, 109
Evans, Wayne, 137
evolution, 88-90, 109, 155

Felföldy, Lajos, 82
fertilisers, 80, 81, 82, 173
fossil fuels, 166
fossils, 52, 54, 109

Gaia: acid rain, 159, 172; all species acting together, 90; and altruism, 116; brains of, 143, 144; causality and propensity, 119-120; cooperation of living beings, 100; death of, 126; differs from old manifestation, 12; environmental concern, 158-159; environmental regulation, 123; future of, 174; hypotheses, vii-ix, 174; living Earth, 9-13, 15; living organism, vii, 57; living planet, 126; living system, 96-97; magic, myths and pseudoreligions, 3-9, 111, 113-114, 162; a metaphor, 155; misunderstandings, 114; named by Golding, 27; need of humans, 147; new view of world, 84; planetary management, 130; reproduction of, 153-154; scientific concept, 125; self absorbed, 111-113; self-regulation, 159; single entity world, 175; a system, 146; threats to, 162-163
Gay-Lussac, J.L., 73
genetics, 89
geophysicians, 174
geophysiology, 161-162
God, 111, 114, 116
Golding, William, 27
grasses, 140
gravity, 56
Great Barrier Reef, 69, 70
Great Salt Lake, 66
green plants, 52
greenhouse effect, 47-49, 135, 136, 137, 138, 140, 149, 163

halite, 71
haze, 169
helium, 29
Himalayas, 93
Hitchcock, Dian, 26
humans, 87; body system, 96; as Gaian brain, 143; passion for information, 152
Hutton, James, 10, 12
hydrogen, 29, 31, 37, 83
hydrogen bombs, 134
hypothermia, 44

ice, 33

ice ages, 49-50, 55, 135, 139
ice caps, 64, 68
ice sheets, 137
images, 6
information and communication, 151-152
Institute for Chemistry, Mainz, 55
iodine, 72-75, 83
iron, 32

Jurassic period, 50
Jupiter, 18

Korolenko, Yevgraf Maximovich, 11

language, 6
lead, 46
life: absence or presence of, 14-27, 35-39, 126; appears on Earth, 95; collaboration of communities, 109, 116-117; definition of, 14-15, 21; existence on Earth, 90; expectancy of planet, 127; Gaian hypothesis, 174; intelligent, 38-39; proliferation of, 132; purpose of, 142; self-sustaining, 97
limestone, 71
liquids, 22-23
lithium, 29
Living Earth, 9-13
living organisms, 38
Lovelock, James, vii, ix, 10, 19, 21, 23, 26-27, 76, 84, 95, 120, 122, 123, 128, 133, 161

magic, 113-114
mammals, 133
Manchester Literary and Philosophical Society, 171
mantle, 53
Mars, 18, 19, 24, 25, 26, 29, 35, 85, 90, 126, 148; greening of, 147-150
Mediterranean, 67
Mercury, 18, 24
metals, 84

metaphors, 154-156
methane, 36-38, 40, 136, 167
microbial metallurgists, 83-84
Milky Way, 151
Milton, John, 88
minerals, 77
monocultures, 135
Moon, 154
morality, 111-113
Mother Earth, 4-6, 8-9
mountains, 93, 94
mythological aspects, viii, 113-114

NASA, 19
natural selection, 110
neutrons, 30, 31
nickel, 32
nitrates, 173
nitrogen, 33-35, 36, 42-43, 83, 174
North American Space Agency see NASA
North Sea, 138
nuclear power, 165-167
nutrients, 81, 82-83

oceans, 129, 139, 163; size of, 56-57
organic matter, 84
organisms, 41, 51, 53, 57, 68, 70, 77, 84, 104, 108, 109, 116, 120, 128, 145, 155
The Origin of the Species, 98, 99
osmosis, 62
oxygen, 28-29, 35-36, 37, 78, 83; dangers of, 39-41; uses for, 41
ozone layer, 11, 167-170

Pacific atolls, 134
Paradise Lost, 88
Pennines, 72
pesticides, 11
phenomena, 157
phosphorus, 82, 83
photosynthesis, 35, 40, 52, 54, 56, 69, 85, 131, 134, 140
physical world, 86-87
physics, 21
Planck, Max, 55

planets: balance of, 137-139; death of, 126-141; humans visiting, 151; injuring, 146; life and death of, 126-141; life detector, 23-24; living, 43; physicians to, 157-175; searching for life on, 14-27; supporting life, 22-23, 154
plankton, 80
plants, 40, 41, 85, 147; analysis of, 81; death of, 128-130; marine, 82
Plósz, Sándor, 82
pollution, 41, 131, 136, 162-163
polyps, 69, 70
Popper, Sir Karl, 119
prokaryotes, 108, 147
proteins, 76
protons, 30, 31
pseudoreligions, 113-114

radiation, 48, 73, 136, 138
radioactive Earth, 47
radiometric dating, 46
Rapoport, Anatol, 118
recycling information, 75-76
Red Sea, 64
riddles, 1, 2, 3, 14
rock, 10
rocks, 45, 56; and fossils, 52; dating of, 46-47; sedimentary, 45, 55
Royal Society of Edinburgh, 10

salinity, 64, 65, 71, 79, 96
salt, 59-60
Salt Lake (Utah), 60
Salt Sea, 59
samarium, 47
Satan, 88
Saturn, 18
Schidlowski, Manfred, 55
science, practice of, 2
Sea of Azov, 67
sea: bed, 51-52; and carbon cycle, 54; not frozen, 44-45; water, 44, 58-71, 68; wave power, 165
seals, 143

Search for Extraterrestrial Intelligence (SETI), 18
seaweed, 75, 79-80
sedimentary rocks, 45, 55
sediments, 51, 70, 77, 93
self-regulation, 129
Siberian Institute of Technology, 132
sky, 21-23; why it is blue, 28-29
Smith, R.S., 171
snakes, 102
snow, 49, 50
social behaviour, 143
Socrates, 142
sodium, 59
solar system, 24, 29, 43, 46, 85, 90, 126-127, 133, 151; formation of, 32-33; life in, 18-19
Sonea, Sorin, 106
South Pole, 168
space programme, 16
space ventures, 150-151
Spaceship Earth, 87-88, 90, 92
Spencer, Herbert, 99, 100, 102
Sputnik 1, 16
stability, 124-125
stars: birth and death of, 29-32; gazing, 16; travel, 151
Stickstoff (German for nitrogen), 42
strontium, 47
sulphur, 76-80, 83, 172
Sun, 29, 32, 33, 44, 45, 48, 85, 91, 95, 127, 129
suplhur, 83
survival of the fittest, 99-100

tectonics, 93
teleology, 114, 123, 154
temperature, 22, 42, 43, 48, 53, 55, 95, 97, 111, 136, 138, 139, 168
Tennyson, 98, 102
termites, 132
thorium, 46
thyroid, 74
thyroxin, 72-74
Tibet, 22, 42
tit for tat theory, 117-119

toxic industrial waste, 160
trees, 76
Tyndall, John, 48

University of Michigan, 117
University of Toronto, 118
uranium, 46

Venus, 18, 19, 24, 25, 29, 35, 85,
    90, 91, 126
Vernadsky, Vladimir, 11
Viking spacecraft, 26
violence, 103, 104
Virgin Mary, 7
volcanoes, 33, 47, 53, 82, 90, 93, 129
von Liebig, Justus, 81
Vostok station, 49

The War of the Worlds, 19
water, 47; fresh, 64
water cycle, 83
water vapour, 33, 138
Wells, H.G., 19
whales, 159
Williams, Tennessee, 87
wind generators, 164
Wittner, Ilona, 82
World Philosophy Conference,
    119
world, divided, 86-87

Xanthippe, 142

zooxanthellae, 69